Digital Citizenship in the 21ˢᵗ Century

The Fielding Monograph Series is published by Fielding Graduate University,
2020 De la Vina Street, Santa Barbara, CA 93105.
Phone: (805) 898-2924. Fax: (805) 690-4310. On the web: www.fielding.edu.

Fielding Monograph Series

Digital Citizenship in the 21st Century

Volume 7

Edited by
Jason Ohler, PhD

TABLE OF CONTENTS

INTRODUCTION

For many of us, living in two places at once is our new home. First, we live in real life, or RL as we now refer to it. Once simply referred to as "life," we have had to rename it in order to distinguish it from the second place we now live, IR, or immersive reality, which we experience through the screens that connect us to the world on the other end of our smart devices. Our devices are, to quote MIT's Sherry Turkle, "always on and always on us," providing us with access to a secondary source of information, and a secondary sense of place, wherever we are. We could return to our RL roots by simply turning off our devices. But few of us will actually do so. Being always connected, and living a "duotaneous" life, is the new normal.

We accepted our parallel virtual existence quickly and en masse, which led to the development of common virtual space and the formation of on-line communities. This, in turn, made us wonder what it meant to belong to those communities in terms of behavior and social norms. From these interests emerged "digital citizenship," a field of inquiry that addresses our expectations, concerns, and hopes about living in our two realities, as well as about blending the two into one integrated, healthy approach to living.

As we pioneered new lands in virtual reality it became clear that using existing standards of citizenship would offer only limited perspectives in terms of helping us understand our second lives. We were literally rein-venting ourselves in virtual space, and creating new worlds that spanned traditional and online communities. Clearly, we needed new research to inform our efforts. Researchers, driven both by intense curiosity as well as by a genuine interest in humanizing our new spaces, have accepted the challenge of illuminating our new adventures in social evolution.

This monograph features the work of six researchers from the Field-ing Media Psychology program who have helped illuminate the world of digital citizenship and social change. Each has approached research from a very different perspective.

The monograph begins with a consideration of how large group narrative is unconsciously constructed using social media. Dr. Michael Neal considered how narrative forms emerged from a large-scale Twitter feed, in order to see how a real life event, in this case a Republican convention, was repurposed into narrative expression using one channel of our second world, in this case Twitter.

Dr. Jenny Fremlin considers the sense of community that participants feel across multiple communities spanning real life and immersive reality. Her study of World of WarCraft users asked participants to explore, compare, and contrast their sense of community in their local neighborhood, an online community, their online gaming team, and a community of choice.

Dr. Yashica Holmes-Smith examines teens' perceptions of living media saturated lifestyles. From her work we gain an in-depth consideration of the world of teenagers who are growing up fully acclimated to living two places at once.

Dr. Christophe Morin, a leader in consumer neuroscience, considers the specific impacts of one kind of media message, the PSA, on the lives of young people. In particular he was interested in how brain-based persuasion models might explain the success or demise of many public health campaigns.

Dr. Deirdre Bradley addresses aspects of the gender digital divide and empowerment of women through mobile technology, particularly in underserved populations.

Dr. Jon Cabiria's research addresses the interplay of our two worlds in terms of personal identity. His research sought to understand the experiences of selected lesbian and gay participants in their online social activities, and to discover whether positive benefits experienced online were transferrable to real-world lives.

Taken together, the content of this volume provide a broad base of research about our lives as digital citizens, and the social change that has developed because of the two places we now live. Readers are invited to read this work and then ponder the question that all of us are asking these days, in one form or another: Just what does it mean to be a digital citizen?

We wish to thank those members of the Fielding Media Psychology faculty who reviewed the work included in this monograph. They are Dr. Regina Tuma, Dr. Pamela Rutledge, Dr. Karen Dill-Shackleford, Dr. Garry Hare, and Dr. Jean-Pierre Isbouts.

JASON OHLER, PHD, EDITOR
KRISTIAN ALOMA, EDITORIAL COORDINATOR

GROUP CONSTRUCTED NARRATIVES ON TWITTER

Michael Neal, PhD, Fielding Graduate University, USA
In memoriam

A Special Note from the Editor

Dr. Michael Neal completed his PhD in Media Psychology in Spring, 2013. Tragically, he passed away a short time later. With permission from his wife Teresa, I asked Kristian Aloma to prepare his research for this monograph. My thanks to Kristian for his hard work, to Teresa for her understanding, and to Dr. Michael Neal for his brilliant research.

Abstract: The emergence of social media as a communication platform is changing the way members of society connect to and exchange information with each other. These new connections allow individuals around the world to document and comment on social events in real time as participants, observers and, in some cases, both. This research explored whether a loosely created, short-lived social group discussing a single topic constructs narratives. The research demonstrated that a large group of Twitter users is capable of generating narrative during a live event without the organized intent to do so. The implications suggest that story making happens "naturally," not only for individuals but for groups, and that narrative is perhaps the foundational schema we use to organize our personal and social experience. The research also suggests that society should be concerned about how social media conversations can be fabricated or skewed, distorting our sense of history.

Keywords: Twitter, narrative construction, storytelling, collective memory, storytelling elements, narrative knowing, Republican National Convention, storytelling traditions, information use theory, ontology in mental models, social network data analysis, technical media content analysis

Introduction

In 2012, Facebook claimed 955 million active users (Facebook, 2012). Typically, Facebook users provide regular status updates that chronicle their life events, whether they are significant or mundane. LinkedIn boasts 175 million reported members through its networking site, which provides a professional presence for those wanting to share their work history and educational achievements (LinkedIn, 2014). The micro-blogging site Twitter had an estimated 500 million users during the same time period (Dugan, 2012). Twitter is used for a variety of purposes, including journaling, documenting and commenting on major events as they occur, following people and topics of interest, and much more. The nature of these tweets and the purposes for which they are used are certainly important. But also important is their size, because the formation of dynamic social groups, the construction of knowledge, and the chronicling of historical events all become possible on a much larger scale than ever before in history.

Note that the utility of each of the social media network sites mentioned above is rooted in storytelling, which is the central component of memory, meaning making, and communication among social groups (e.g., Laszlo, 2009; Polkinghorne, 1988). The purpose of this research was to explore a large-scale Twitter event as a story. In particular, this research explored whether such an event would conform to conventional story forms organically, without the benefit of preplanning or defined authorship. Twitter was selected as a subject of study because of the near real-time nature with which it is used to chronicle an actual event. The shrinking delay between real-time events and our response to them using a service such as Twitter makes analyzing the construction of narrative in social media important to understand.

Large social groups have created political movements that use Twitter as a communication platform. In 2011, a very large demonstration occurred in Tahrir Square in Cairo, Egypt. This was associated with the Arab Spring movement, as it was known in popular media, which was a network of widespread protests across the Arab world. One of the most notable aspects of the protests in Tahrir Square was the role of social media in the event. Protesters used social media sites to quickly arrange, organize, and reorganize the protests. Additionally, the same social media sites were used to report on the protest. For the first time in history, the world had access to an international event directly from its participants, as opposed to reporters on location whose news feeds had to be channeled through major network news stations, often on a delayed basis. The protesters, and those observing the demonstration from all over the world, turned Twitter into a real-time report on the happenings of Tahrir Square. Protesters could share stories that invited audience participation. To formally document the protests, Alex Nunns and Nadia Idle wrote a book titled *Tweets from Tahrir: Egypt's Revolution as It Unfolded in the Words of the People Who Made It* (2011). It is important to note that the Tahrir Square protests are just one example of using Twitter to chronicle a real-time event and organize its participants as well as engage the public (e.g., Gambs, 2012; Hossmann, Legendre, & Carta, 2011; Hughes & Palen, 2009; Li & Rao, 2010; Nunns & Idle, 2011).

Events such as the mass tweeting that happened in Tahrir Square invite our inquiry. Have those who use social media in these kinds of situations taken on the responsibility of historian? How accurate are their portrayals of such events? Might the formal description of an event now be in the hands of an audience experiencing it live instead of an historian writing about it months after it took place, with the benefit of background research and reflection? In addition, what checks are in place to ensure that the stories that might be created via social media are accurate and ethically responsible?

Consider the story of Justine Sacco, reported by Jon Ronson in *The New York Times Magazine*. In 2013, she was a young public relations senior director and a fledgling user of Twitter with 170 followers. She was making a connection through London Heathrow Airport on her way to South Africa when she published a tweet that said "Going to Africa. Hope I don't get AIDS. Just kidding. I'm white!" Ronson described it as a stupid tweet, but it became one that would eventually be interpreted and judged without Sacco ever standing in the defendant's box. At first, nothing came of the tweet. Sacco was well into her flight to South Africa without access to the Internet when her tweet was forwarded to a reporter for Gawker by one of her followers; the reporter retweeted it to a network of thousands of followers. Over the next 11 hours of Sacco's flight, she became a top trending topic on Twitter, meaning she was one of the most frequent topics of tweets across the entire Twitter network. The content of the tweets ranged from ridicule to disgust and included revealing private information, a link to the airline and flight number of Sacco's flight, and calls for physical and sexual violence against her. Ronson described the tsunami of commentary on Twitter as a "furor . . . Her complete ignorance of her predicament for those 11 hours lent the episode both dramatic irony and a pleasing narrative arc" (Ronson, 2015).

With traditional publications, there is often a single identifiable author of the content. However, in the age of social media, where the group both creates and consumes the narratives that rise within its system, the line between author and audience blurs. Who bears the responsibility for the trial by public narrative that someone like Sacco might experience? What impact do these interactive narratives have on the psychological experience of those involved in them? It is questions like these that should be of particular interest for media psychology.

Statement of the Problem

The investigator's original research, and this essay, examine whether a loosely created, informal, and often short-lived social group discussing or commenting on a single topic can construct cogent, meaningful narratives based on recognized storytelling principles. If they do, this will suggest that the event being observed, in this case the 2012 Republican National Convention, evokes the psychological aspects of narrative knowledge creation. This research asks whether there are elements of traditional storytelling found in the construction of a narrative for a specific event through social media micro-blogs. The investigator hypothesized, and confirmed, that there will be structural elements of storytelling in an analysis of the micro-blog Twitter during the Republican National Convention. A specific subset of over 200,000 tweets was analyzed. This analysis was conducted from the perspective of information use theory (R.S. Taylor, 1991) regarding the dynamic formation of social groups and traditional storytelling. The study was conducted using the Twitter streams covering the 2012 Republican National Convention. Leximancer, a sentiment and concept-based qualitative analysis software program, was used to analyze the data.

Conceptual Framing

There are three primary areas of theory that provide the path to answering these research questions: 1) narrative tradition and structure; 2) social group dynamics; and 3) social media communication. Each is addressed in turn.

The existing literature in narrative tradition and structure focuses substantially on descriptions of storytelling and narrative knowledge construction (e.g., Ohler, 2007; Polkinghorne, 1988; Roland & Duisit, 1975). However, very little of that literature examines social media analysis rooted in communication use theory. Even less focus is given to narrative knowing and social construction of narrative. Analyzing the content from Twitter depends on first identifying which narrative framework to use to conduct the analysis.

While the world is extremely familiar with story, it is our familiarity with it that sometimes makes it so difficult to study and understand. As a consequence, there exists no clear, consistent, or satisfying definition of a story in the social sciences. We have evidence of human beings telling stories since the 11th century BCE (Isbouts & Ohler, 2013). We also know that stories are used throughout a person's daily activities (Polkinghorne, 1988) and that there are many formats and situations in which stories manifest themselves, including fiction versus nonfiction, stories with children, songs, and blogs. Yet we still have no clearly articulated sense of what makes a story a story. In order to provide a theoretical foundation for his work, the investigator studied major contributors to narrative research and developed the following summary table that identified the variables of narrative (Adams, 2007; Aristotle, 2012; Barthes & Duisit, 1975; Bickham, 1997; Bruce, 1978; Campbell, 2008/1949; Chatman, 1980; Egan, 1986;

Haven, 2007; Mandler & Johnson, 1977; McKee, 1997; Ohler, 2007; Propp, 2009/1958; Simmons, 2006):

Table 1
Key Components of Story Structure

Author	Key Components of Story Structure
Adams	Beginning, first significant event, middle, climax, end
Aristotle	Plot is primary; middle, beginning, end; optional characters
Barthes & Duisit	Functions (unit of content), actions, narration, (discourse) as a hierarchical organization
Bickham	Basic plot, name and viewpoint of main character (protagonist), protagonist's goal, antagonist's goal and how he or she opposes the protagonist, scene development, viewpoint, change
Bruce	Plot, character, setting, continuity, conflict, connectivity
Campbell	Call to adventure, helpers, tests, helpers, flight, elixir
Chatman	Events (actions, happening), existences (characters, settling)
Egan	Clear beginning and end, binary opposites, rhythm of expectation and satisfaction, concern with affective responses
Haven	Character, intent (goal and motive), actions, struggles, details (characters, settings, events)
Mandler & Johnson	Settings, beginnings, reactions, attempts and actions, outcomes, endings

McKee	Events from characters' life stories, strategic sequence, arousal of emotions, express view of life
Ohler	Beginning, central challenge, character transformation, resolution of challenge
Propp	Initial situation, 31 functions (actions or events that occur)
Simmons	Detail, characters, events, points of view

The table, and an analysis of each author's definition of a story, reveals some common elements that most agree are a critical, or primary, part of a story:
- Beginning: The start of the story
- Protagonist: The main character of the story
- Setting: The location and/or environment where the story occurs
- Temporal element: A sense of passing time
- Problem Definition: The problem facing the protagonist
- Ending/Conflict Resolution: Resolution of the problem in some manner

The summary above was used during the research to indicate the required elements for a story. This became the investigator's coding matrix. However, additional elements of story were also identified and these were added to the coding matrix to allow for additional interpretation and exploration of themes:
- Antagonist: An opposing force to the protagonist; may be an actual person or cause of conflict
- Supporting Characters: Characters who support the protagonist
- Transformation: A change that occurs in the protagonist or problem

Polkinghorne suggested that, out of a narrative, we should find an understandable composite. This will become a single storyline that links actions and events through plot (1988). Thus, when a social group creates a narrative, we would expect a single, unifying plotline to emerge. However, Twitter users are an asynchronous group composing a narrative both together and separately. As such, there is a possibility that a single plotline will diverge into multiple courses of action. We find a potential resolution in Polkinghorne, who elaborated that "a plot has the capability to articulate and consolidate complex threads of multiple activities by means of the overlay of multiple subplots" (1988, p. 19). This research focused on both the initial and emergent plotlines.

As a group, human beings naturally created meaning of their lives through stories (Polkinghorne, 1988). However, when exploring whether individuals on Twitter create stories, we must first explore whether unrelated users of the Twitter site form groups in the first place. Within social group dynamics, the theories that appeared most relevant here included ideas around shared experience, social representation theory, reception theory, and selective exposure and homophily. The literature about shared experience provides insight into how senders and receivers of narratives process and experience stories. Shared experiences are important to this research because the coherence of the message is critical to constructing and consuming the narrative. The narrative must also represent, at some level, a shared reality in order to create coherence. The integrations and creation of a shared reality have a social and cultural aspect. At a cultural level, narratives can provide cohesion for shared beliefs and transmit a message producer's values to the group at large (Barthes, 1977).

Wagner et al. (1999) defined social representations with regards to a community as a collective experience created by individuals from the group through daily conversations. This suggests how social media could use representations for the development of a group narrative. According to Moscovici (1984), individuals create representations in the course of communication and cooperation, and meaning is created through this discourse. Social representations are formed from language, culture, and history. Therefore, finding narratives from the group of users on Twitter would suggest that the group is also producing social representations as well.

What is unique about Twitter is the role in which the author is both reader and author. Using reception theory, we look at this idea more closely. First, the most important party in a narrative, in many regards, is not the storyteller but rather the audience. Barthes (1977) emphasized the importance of the audience:

> Thus revealed the total existence of writing: a text is made of multiple writings, from many cultures and entering into mutual relations of dialogue, parody, contestation, but there is one place where this multiplicity is focused and that place is the reader, not, as was hitherto said, the author. The reader is the space on which all the quotations that make up a writing are inscribed without any of them being lost; a text's unity lies not in its origin but in its destination. (p. 148)

On Twitter, as stated, there are authors, readers (information consumers), and reader-author combinations. When readers become authors, reception theory becomes critical as to how their interpretation of what they read will affect their own future writing and their impact on the narrative itself.

Another implication of the authoring is mixing fiction and nonfiction elements of the event, either intentionally or unintentionally. Whether the story being consumed is fiction or nonfiction, fictional elements will still appear as a result of the authorship and consumption of the story. Haven (2007) explains:

> Nonfiction is not equal to truth and reality. The act of picking specific language, of including or excluding specific events and details, and of organizing the material into a flowing narrative sequence automatically fictionalizes the story by adding perspective, viewpoint, attitude, and belief. (p. 128)

As a result, the authors of the narrative that emerges from a Twitter conversation regarding an event may also influence the receiver's perception of the event based on what content they include, exclude, or create in their tweets.

The theory of selective exposure plays an important role here. Festinger (1957) postulated that people are resistant to changing what does not fit well with their existing beliefs. Simmons (2006) said it simply as, "People interpret facts to mean what their story tells them they mean" (p. 53).

Given the apparently natural, human inclination to gravitate to particular people and narratives, it seems reasonable to assume that Twitter users are most often seeking out the opinions of those whose opinions are similar to their own. People interact with similar people at higher rates than dissimilar people (McPherson et al., 2001).

However, homophily may be challenged in a social network such as Twitter. Yardi and Boyd (2010) found that an event centered around a Twitter hashtag cannot guarantee, and may even discourage homophily, because of the ability of any user to add commentary, opinion, humor, or alternative plotlines to the discussion of the event via use of the hashtag. As such, the investigator expected to find that the narratives created by the users on Twitter may not reflect, and in some cases may directly contradict, the narrative desired by the event being observed.

In the literature related to social media communication, research has found that computer mediated communication (CMC) conversations online are captured and recorded, which makes up for the lack of continuity in an asynchronous conversation (Herring, 1999). Herring noted that messages on a computer-mediated platform can also be dysfunctional and incoherent but that users of the system have evolved ways of signaling to each other to know when it's their time to take a turn (Herring, 1999). This seems improbably on Twitter, in which thousands of tweets are streamed per minute. Turn-taking and synchronous processing of messages is impossible. Therefore, conversations, sharing, and processing of information take place in new ways, which sometimes skip new messages entirely. These aspects of a mass Twitter event create a different communication environment than has previously been studied.

Yet some evidence already exists that suggests narrative participation among a Twitter group mimics traditional knowledge construction among a group having a standard conversation (Polichak & Gerrig, 2002). Polichak and Gerrig (2002) found that Twitter users took a side-participant role, which improved the coherence of the narrative and impacted the processing of those same narratives. Participating in the Twitter conversation affected user emotions and memory, impacted beliefs, and changed beliefs because of the narrative participation.

To summarize, a review of the literature revealed that common story elements do exist and will inform the coding matrix used in this study. In addition, if narratives are present among the group, we should also find evidence of them via social group dynamics, including how the participants interact with social media and how groups use social events to communicate about an event. The group should create common social representations of different ideas related to the event. In addition, the establishing of a group around an event will influence the narratives that are generated by the groups, whether they are consistent with or contradictory to the intended narrative of the event. All of this will also take place within a context of social media communication and be influenced by the nature of computer-mediated communications, in which synchronization, the development of grammar, and other techniques to manage the abundance of data contributed to the data will be leveraged by the participants and impact the narrative created.

To explore this, the study will leverage the story elements ontology synthesized from the 14 scholars reviewed.

In addition to using Leximancer to analyze data, this study also used a grounded theory examination of the text to identify concepts within the texts. Narrative analysis of the content was used to identify narrative elements and connections. A discourse analysis explored the temporal components not necessarily related to story timeline, societal power structures, relationships between people and institutions, and the emotions, practices, and material conditions of the content.

Findings

The study required three steps in order to analyze whether group-created narratives are indeed present on Twitter. First, the investigator collected Twitter data related to the Republican National Convention that occurred in 2012. The event's official hashtag, #GOP2012 (Twitter, 2012), was used to filter the tweets. The actual data were gathered using the DiscoverText collection service (http://www.discovertext.com) with access to the GNIP

Full Twitter Pipe. In total, 225,205 tweets were collected for analysis. The data were analyzed using the Leximancer software program (Smith, 2012) and automatically coded concepts from the text. In addition to its thorough text analytics, Leximancer uses statistics-based algorithms for analysis to produce several quantitative measures. Challenges related to content from Twitter included the unique grammatical rules used by Twitter users and different types of syntax specific to the social network. Decisions were carefully made in Leximancer to compensate for these challenges.

The second step was to use the story ontology coding matrix that was developed to identify the presence or absence of components of narrative. Table 2 was used for this purpose. It includes three columns that identify and explain each story element, as well as providing an identifying code. Elements were coded as either Required ("R") or Supporting ("S"). Required elements were defined as those needed to ensure the presence of a complete narrative. Supporting elements were defined as those used to quantitatively measure the richness of the added elements. All other elements were designated "O" for "Other" because they did not fit into a required or supporting role for the narrative.

Table 2

Story Element Ontology for the Study

Rating	Story Element	Description
R	Beginning	The start of the story
R	Protagonist	The main character that the story is about
S	Antagonist	A force opposing the protagonist; may be either another character or a cause of conflict
R	Setting	Location and/or environment where the story occurs
S	Supporting Characters	Characters that support the protagonist
R	Temporal Element	A sense of passing time

R	Problem Definition	The problem facing the protagonist
S	Transformation	A change that occurs in the protagonist or problem
R	Ending/Conflict Resolution	The problem is resolved in some manner
O	Other	Concepts that do not fit into any other elements

Note: The concepts generated by Leximancer were manually coded using the above matrix

The third step of the study was to determine a quantitative measure for coverage of story elements. Once coded, the concepts were measured for actual coverage of the story elements ontology. This measure demonstrated the completeness of the narrative elements and determined whether a narrative existed or not.

Three storylines from the 2012 Republican National Convention are discussed in the investigator's research and all relate to the theme of this monograph—Digital Citizenship for Social Change. The first was a storyline that emerged related to Mitt Romney. The second was a storyline related to Clint Eastwood and an empty chair. The third was a plotline related to but disconnected from Ann Romney.

"Mitt Romney" was the most common concept related to the convention. The storyline focused on the formal nomination of Mitt Romney throughout the initial days of the convention. Table 3 maps the story elements of this plotline.

Table 3

Story Element Mapping of Story Plotline "Mitt Romney"

Rating	Concept	Story Element	Notes
R	BREAKING	Beginning	Speech started
R	Romney	Protagonist	Nominee: Romney

S	Ron Paul	Antagonist	Opponent in primary; supporters vocal during vote counts
S	Ryan and variants Ann Romney	Supporting Character	Vice Presidential Nominee Wife of Nominee
R	Today Votes	Temporal Element	When votes will be tallied Long process to officially determine nominee
R	Convention	Setting	Where the nomination and voting takes place
R	Nomination Campaign	Problem Definition	The goal of the comparison and nomination process
S	Nominee	Transformation	Romney moves from GOP primary campaigner to GOP nominee
R	Celebrate	Conflict Resolution	Convention attendees celebrate nomination and end of the transformation

The results of the coding showed coverage of all required story elements and demonstrated that the required narrative elements formed a complete storyline. This confirms the hypothesis that a narrative was expected to emerge from the tweets originating from the convention. This is not surprising, given that the event under study had a narrative objective. However, what is interesting to the digital citizen is when narratives are produced that were not intended, or are not in the best interest of society.

Clint Eastwood spoke during the convention and a plotline emerged about him as well. However, analysis found it was perhaps not the plotline intended. Table 4 maps the story elements of this plotline.

Table 4

Story Element Mapping of Story Plotline "Clint Eastwood"

Rating	Concept	Story Element	Notes
R	Speaking	Beginning	Speech started
R	Speaker Mystery guest	Protagonist	Eastwood himself
S	Chair Invisible Obama chair	Antagonist	"Attempted social representation" of President Obama Fictional represen- tation of President Obama
S	Marco (Ru- bio) Mitt Romney	Supporting Char- acter	
R	Day Speaking	Temporal Ele- ment	Speaking on the day of the speech
R	Empty Chair Teleprompter Convention Sad	Setting	Empty chairs at convention; East- wood talked of empty chair
R	Rambling Drunk Weird Senile	Problem Defini- tion	
S	Thismakesm- esadinside	Transformation	Someone get Clint Eastwood Obam- aCare

As with the Mitt Romney plotline analysis, all of the required elements were present and there was a narrative storyline. Three supporting elements were found. The intrigue of this plotline is that it was counter to the message Eastwood was attempting to deliver in his speech. In the results, five concepts out of 50, or 10%, were commentary on Clint Eastwood himself and not the narrative he was telling. This demonstrates what can be called a side-view narrative created to provide a direct commentary and a narrative of someone trying to create a narrative.

Ann Romney spoke at the event in support of her husband, Mitt Romney. While Ann Romney did not become the subject of the plotline as Clint Eastwood did, the narrative that was identified in the Twitter data was not her narrative either. Table 5 maps the story elements of this plotline.

Table 5

Story Element Mapping of Story Plotline "Ann Romney"

Rating	Concept	Story Element
R	Speak	Beginning
R	@hrc	Protagonist
S	Mitt Romney, Republicans	Antagonist
S		Supporting Character
R		Temporal Element
R	In Tampa, Convention	Setting
R	Marriage Equality	Problem Definition
S	Real marriage	Transformation
R	Marriage equality	Conflict Resolution

As with the previous two plotlines, all of the required elements were present. Additionally, three supporting elements were also found. The narrative, however, was emergent and divergent to the narrative Mrs. Romney was attempting to deliver. Out of the data, eight of the concepts out of 50, or 16%, were directly related to the issue of same-sex marriage and marriage equality. The authors and receivers creating the narrative around this event shifted the narrative entirely. Instead of Ann Romney being the protagonist as Mitt Romney and Clint Eastwood were in the narratives related to their speeches, the Human Rights Campaign inspired a new narrative with itself as the protagonist. This narrative became one of protest against the actual event taking place.

Conclusions

With these last two plotlines, we see that the digital citizenry of the convention, using Twitter as its platform, was able to take control of the conversation related to the event and shift the narrative. This was not done by a single author but by the group sharing in the experience of the event. One can assume that it was not Eastwood's intent to be perceived as drunk or senile or for Ann Romney to inspire a narrative related to marriage equality, an issue she opposes. For those not participating or observing the event directly, the narratives produced by Twitter create a history of the event that may be at odds with the intent of the event itself. In so doing, it may then influence the narrative consumed by others after the fact without an ability to verify or confirm the actual events themselves.

The study was particularly interesting because it focused on an event that consisted almost entirely of people giving speeches. This raises questions related to narrative rooting. Were the narratives that emerged those that were intended by the speaker? Or were the narratives that emerged about the person giving the speech? Indeed, we saw a third option present itself in the plotline about Ann Romney when an entirely new, but related, narrative was generated. The Human Rights Campaign's (HRC) marriage equality narrative emerged because of its timing around Ann Romney's speech and its ability to leverage elements of Ann Romney's speech content.

If events such as these had been taking place during a time before social media narratives, might the narratives have shifted so dramatically? The shift of Eastwood's narrative and the hijacking of Mrs. Romney's narrative occurred because of the presence of social networking sites like Twitter. The group was able to use existing narratives to create different, unintended narratives. In so doing, they affected the creation of knowledge by a group of users connected to Twitter. It is the power of the digital citizenry that has most likely inspired governments with a more hostile relationship to independent media to ban social networking sites within their countries. The power of a digital citizenry—especially in countries in which there is little transparency to the world—to control the narrative consumed by that world is formidable.

The research question asked whether there are elements of traditional storytelling found in the construction of a narrative for a specific event through social media micro-blogs, namely Twitter. It was confirmed by the study that narratives do exist among these groups, though they were not always as expected. Twitter users both reflected the narratives of the event and also introduced narratives with different objectives than those that actually occurred at the event.

Recommendations for Future Research

Social media is still a young aspect of the human experience and there is much to learn about its impact on our psychology. Research activity in the social sciences can expand on the research primarily found in the technical computer science community. Investigators should explore the social implications of these new and unique methods of large group communication. The data also revealed that user-created data generates considerable differences in the quality, vernacular, and use of the data. Future research should focus on word usage and intent as well as the content of the data itself as this study did. Finally, the area of narrative transportation theory (Green & Brock, 2002) should be explored further. With the presence of narrative among a group of Twitter users observing a live event, there is the potential that other observers might be psychologically transported to the event through those narratives and have an impact on the persuasion of those events and the narratives being generated around them.

References

Adams, K. (2007). *How to improvise a full-length play: The art of spontaneous theater* [Kindle DX Version]. New York, NY: Allworth

Press.

Barthes, R. (1977). The death of the author. *Image Music Text* (pp. 142-148). London, UK: Fontana.

Barthes, R., & Duisit, L. (1975). An Introduction to the structural analysis of narrative. *New Literary History, 6*(2), 237-272. doi: 10.2307/468419Facebook. (2012).

Bickham, J. (1997). *The 38 most common fiction writing mistakes.* Cincinnati, OH: Writer's Digest Books.

Bruce, B. (1978). What makes a story good? Language Arts, 55, 460-466.

Campbell, J. (2008/1949). *The hero with a thousand faces.* Novato, CA: New World Library.

Chatman, S. (1980). *Story and discourse: Narrative structure in fiction and film.* Ithaca, NY: Cornell University Press.

Dugan, L. (2012). Twitter to surpass 500 million registered users on Wednesday. Retrieved from http://www.mediabistro.com/alltwitter/500-million-registered-users_b18842.

Egan, K. (1986). *Teaching as storytelling: An alternative approach to teaching and curriculum in the elementary school.* Chicago, IL: The University of Chicago Press.

Festinger, L. (1957). *A theory of cognitive dissonance.* Stanford, CA: Stanford University Press.

Gambs, D. (2012). Occupying Social Media. *Socialism and Democracy, 26*(2), 55-60. doi: 10.1080/08854300.2012.686275

Green, M. C., & Brock, T. C. (2002). In the mind's eye: Transportation-imagery model of narrative persuasion. In M. C. Green, J. J. Strange, & T. C. Brock (Eds.), *Narrative impact: Social and cognitive foundations* (pp. 315-341). Mahwah, NJ: Lawrence Erlbaum Associates.

Herring, S. (1999). Interactional coherence in CMC. *Journal of Computer-Mediated Communication, 4*(4). Retrieved from http://dx.doi.org/10.1111/j.1083-6101.1999.tb00106.x.

Hossmann, T., Legendre, F., & Carta, P. (2011). Twitter in disaster mode: Opportunistic communication and distribution of sensor data in emergencies. Paper presented at the Third Extreme Workshop on Communications.

Hughes, A. L., & Palen, L. (2009). Twitter adoption and use in mass convergence and emergency events. *International Journal of Emergency Management, 6*(3), 248-260. doi: 10.1504/ijem.2009.031564

Isbouts, J. & Ohler, J. (In Press). Storytelling and media: Narrative models from Aristotle to augmented reality. In K. E. Dill (Ed.), *Oxford Handbook for Media Psychology*. New York, NY: Oxford Press.

Laszlo, J. (2009). *The science of stories: An introduction to narrative psychology*. London, New York: Routledge.

Li, J., & Rao, H. R. (2010). Twitter as a rapid response news service: An exploration in the context of the 2008 China earthquake. *The Electronic Journal on Information Systems in Developing Countries, 42*(4), 1-22.

LinkedIn. (2012, August 25, 2012). About Us, from http://press.linkedin.com/about.

Mandler, J. M., & Johnson, N. S. (1977). Remembrance of things parsed: Story structure and recall. *Cognitive Psychology, 9*, 111-151.

McKee, R. (1997). *Story*. New York, NY: HarperCollins.

McPherson, M., Smith-Lovin, L., & Cook, J. M. (2001). Birds of a feather: Homophily in social networks. *Annual Review of Sociology*. 27, 415-444.

Moscovici, S. (1984). The phenomenon of social representations. In R. M. Farr & S. Moscovici (Eds.), *Social representations* (pp. 3-69). Cambridge, UK: Cambridge University Press.

Nunns, A., & Idle, N. (Eds.). (2011). *Tweets from Tahrir: Egypt's revolution as it unfolded, in the words of the people who made it*. New York, NY: OR Books.

Ohler, J. (2007). *Digital storytelling in the classroom: New media pathways to literacy, learning, and creativity*. Thousand Oaks, CA: SAGE Publications.

Peck, D. S. (2012). Constructing meaning amidst tragedies within social media groups. (PsyD 3503357), Fielding Graduate University,

United States–California. Dissertations and Theses @ Fielding Graduate University; ProQuest Dissertations & Theses (PQDT) database.

Polichak, J. W., & Gerrig, R. J. (2002). "Get Up and Win!" In M. C. Green, J. J. Strange & T. C. Brock (Eds.), *Narrative Impact: Social and Cognitive Foundations*. Mahwah, NJ: Lawrence Erlbaum Associates.

Polkinghorne, D. E. (1988). *Narrative knowing and the human sciences.* Albany, NY: SUNY Press.

Propp, V. (2009/1958). *Morphology of the folktale.* Austin, TX: University of Texas Press.

Roland, B., & Duisit, L. (1975). An introduction to the structural analysis of narrative. *New Literary History, 6*(2), 237-272.

Ronson, J. (2015). How one stupid tweet blew up Justine Sacco's life. *The New York Times Magazine.* Retrieved from http://www.nytimes. com/2015/02/15/magazine/how-one-stupid-tweet-ruined-justine-saccos-life.html?_r=0.

Simmons, A. (2006). *The story factor: Inspiration, influence, and persuasion through the art of storytelling* [Kindle DX Version]. New York, NY: Basic Books.

Smith, A. (2012). Leximancer (Version 4.0). Brisbane, AU: Leximancer Pty.

Taylor, M., Wells, G., Howell, G., & Raphael, B. (2012). The role of social media as psychological first aid as a support to community resilience building. *Australian Journal of Emergency Management, 27*(1), 20-26.

Taylor, R. S. (1991). Information use environments. In B. Dervin & M. Voight (Eds.), *Progress in Information Sciences* (Vol. 10, pp. 217-255). Norwood, NJ: Ablex.

Twitter. (2011). Twitter help center, from http://support.twitter. com/groups/31-twitter-basics/topics/109-tweets-messages/ articles/127856-about-tweets-twitter-updates.

Wagner, W., Farr, R., Jovchelovitch, S., Lorenzi-Cioldi, F., Marková, I.,

Duveen, G., & Rose, D. (1999). Theory and method of social representations. *Asian Journal of Social Psychology, 2*(1), 95-125.

Yardi, S., & Boyd, D. (2010). Dynamic debates: an analysis of group po-
larization over time on Twitter. *Bulletin of Science, Technology &
Society, 30*(5), 316-327.

CONNECTIONS, TRADITIONAL FACTORS, AND DIGITAL CITIZENSHIP: AN EXPLORATION OF THE SENSE OF COMMUNITY ONLINE AND OFFLINE

J.W. Fremlin, PhD, Fielding Graduate University, USA

Abstract: The psychological sense of community and the factors that build it are well established in research on traditional communities. As society has adopted the everyday use of technology, communities have evolved to both exist in digital spaces and to integrate digital connections with physical communities. Although some research has addressed the presence of a sense of community in online communities, very little has compared it across online communities. In the limited cases where online communities have been approached from a quantitative perspective, the use of unique scales left existing scales untested within online communities and made comparisons between communities challenging. While there is growing interest in the study of online communities and awareness of the presence of a sense of community within them, there has been no agreement on how to measure it, much less how to compare similarities and difference across communities. In an attempt to bridge the study of online and offline communities, this study gathered survey data using the Brief Sense of Community Scale and open-ended responses to compare the sense of community participants felt across multiple communities. Results indicate that there are differences in the sense of community felt in online communities as well as similarities in how sense of community is defined across online and offline communities.

Keywords: sense of community, online communities, Brief Sense of Community Scale, digital connections, MMOG, *World of Warcraft*, neighborhood, digital citizenship

Introduction

As individuals and communities we are still learning the best ways to behave and interact in a world with no physical boundaries. Changes bring about fears of community decline and concerns over new ways of connecting, but at the same time we continue to make new connections through our evolving technology. As we explore communities past and present, research continues to find that these connections offer us some very important benefits. A sense of community has been found to impact overall life satisfaction, efficacy, personal and political trust, mental health, physical health, and economic prosperity (Anderson, 2010; Chavis & Pretty, 1999; Peterson, Speer, & McMillan, 2008; Prezza, Amici, Roberti, & Tedeschi, 2001; Shinn & Toohey, 2002). The ways in which we access our communities and fulfill our needs for community connections are changing, though. It is no longer enough simply to address how we behave and connect online; we also need to understand the similarities and differences in community interactions. As our connections have become increasingly easy to access with mobile, always-on devices we have more than bridged our online and offline interactions—we have interwoven them into one society where we can connect with anyone, anywhere in the world in just four hops (Backstrom, Boldi, Rosa, Ugander, & Vigna, 2012). With these quick connections come new challenges, new ethics, and new relationships. Digital citizenship may have its origins in online behaviors and interactions but, like a sense of community, it is evolving to address the way our modern lives encompass both online and offline information, interactions, and relationships.

When researchers began looking at online communities, one of the first steps was to determine whether online interactions would be similar to offline connections in their support for relationships. The question was: Are online communities really communities? These early studies showed that online communities did offer support and build connections (Hoffman, 2008). Studies even found that connecting a local community with digital support could strengthen it, with online connections playing a role in both local and distant relationships (Hampton, 2001).

However, a sense of community was not directly addressed in a way that made it possible to compare online communities to one another or to offline communities. Most of the studies looked at social cohesion, used qualitative methods, or created new sense-of-community factors specific to the online communities being studied. In the limited cases where online communities were approached from a quantitative perspective, the use of unique scales left existing scales untested within online communities and made comparisons between communities challenging. While our technologically evolving society drives more interest to the study of online communities, and increases awareness of the presence of a sense of community within them, there has been no agreement on how to measure a sense of community much less how to compare the similarities and difference across communities. In an attempt to bridge the study of online and offline communities, this study gathered survey data using the Brief Sense of Community Scale (BSCS) and open-ended responses to compare the sense of community participants felt across multiple communities.

Online Communities Are Not All the Same

In the years since this study was originally published, much has changed in the way that online interactions and mediated communities are seen. A lot of the change has to do with the widespread popularity of digital connections, thanks in large part to our ever-present mobile devices. There is no longer a question of whether an online community or resource can support our everyday lives when we can "phone a friend"—or rather all of our friends at once—through a social network to crowd-source an answer to a trivia question. The answer, like that of the trivia question, is immediate and undeniable. We can be connected at all times in both realms, the digital and the physical. Online and offline, and everything that lies in between, have become our reality.

However, when this research was conducted the literature review revealed that despite growing public discussions about online sense of community, there was very weak support in past research for the application of quantitative scales of a sense of community across online and offline communities. There were theories stating that online communities functioned in a manner similar to traditional communities. There were even a few qualitative studies where members of online communities identified many of the same traditional factors of a sense of community within their online communities and spoke highly of the support they received from online communities. However, in the limited cases where online communities had been approached from a quantitative perspective new scales were developed to address what the researchers saw as major differences in how online and offline communities engaged and supported their members. By using new scales, not only were the existing scales left untested within online communities, but there was also no way to compare the sense of community in an online community to that in an offline community across studies. To make matters more complex, most studies tested unique scales for online communities, making even a comparison of two online communities difficult across studies. It seemed that while there was agreement as to the importance of online communities and the presence of a sense of community within them, there was no agreement on how to measure it much less how to compare the similarities and differences across communities.

Theory and qualitative research showed support for what seemed to be obvious. When people connect with one another in communities the method of that connection, and the technological level of the medium being used to connect, may shape the time it takes to make the connection or the amount of imagination involved in processing the information, but it does not fundamentally change the connections (Obst & Starfurik, 2010; Obst, Zinkiewicz, & Smith, 2002; Prohn, 2009; Roberts, Smith, & Pollock, 2002). However, despite the beginnings of support for digitally-connected communities offering a sense of community similar to those founded offline, what very few studies acknowledged was that there would be differences between the online communities.

One cannot simply say that online communities offer a sense of community and be done with it. Just as traditional communities, formed in physical spaces, differ in their impact on members, the sense of community within an online community can be positive, neutral, or negative (Brodsky, Loomis, & Marx, 2002). Additionally, online communities can offer strong or weak support, and they can thrive or fail. The outcome does not come down to their online nature alone. There are many factors that can play a role in a community's success or failure. Four categories have been identified to encompass those factors. As outlined in the theory of sense of community and used to measure sense of community, they are identified as Shared Emotional Connection, Membership, Influence, and Integration and Fulfillment of Needs (McMillan & Chavis, 1986). These four traditional factors are what the current study set out to compare across multiple communities, spanning both online and offline connections.

In an attempt to begin bridging an examination of online and offline communities, the study gathered survey data using the BSCS and open-ended responses to compare the sense of community that participants felt across multiple communities. To enable comparisons, the same group of participants answered questions about four different communities to which they belonged. Two were predetermined: the online gaming group that was invited to participate in the study and the participant's local neighborhood. Participants chose the other two communities, with one labeled as an online community and the other as a community of choice with no limitations included in the survey.

Method

Two research questions were addressed:

Q1: Can a scale measuring the traditional four factors of sense of community (Shared Emotional Connection, Membership, Influence, and Integration and Fulfillment of Needs) be used to measure sense of community in online communities?

Q2: How do participants characterize sense of community online and offline?

The Sample

This study began with a look at the sense of community that members felt within an online gaming guild, or team of players, in the massive multiplayer online game *World of Warcraft*. The same players then explored their sense of community in their local neighborhood, an online community, and a community of choice. In each community they answered not only survey questions from a traditional quantitative scale of sense of community, but also open-ended questions where they explained their own feelings of sense of community within each community.

The researcher and a research assistant recruited participants using a combination of snowball sampling, through email and social posts, and direct invitations sent to 100 guilds using in-game mail, private in-game chat messages, and posts on guild forums when possible. A total of 77 participants completed the survey. Reddit, where an invitation was shared in two forums, drove the highest number of participants to the study, with 69% of responses (53 participants) completing the survey from a Reddit link. Other participants came from email invitations (12%), guild invitations (8%), and Facebook posts (6%), with the remaining 5% from website and forum posts combined.

Demographics

Participants were mostly male (60%), identified as Caucasian/white (65%), and in the age group 18-24 (45%). They averaged 19.6 hours of game time per week, with an average of 4.2 years playing *World of Warcraft*, and belonged to an average of 1.6 guilds.

Measure/Instrument

Participants answered a demographic questionnaire including these predictors of sense of community from past research: gender; age; ethnicity; income; education; marital status; length of community membership; and time participating in the community. To measure sense of community within each of the four communities identified, participants responded to the eight-item BSCS. The BSCS is a short, validated measure addressing the four traditional factors of sense of community with two positively worded items for each factor. All items use a five-item Likert-type scale. Additionally, the lead author of the sense of community theory who identified the four factors also developed the BSCS. An exploratory single item was included to identify the overall sense of community that participants felt with a five-item Likert-type scale matching the BSCS scale. One item was included for each community in order to measure contact frequency between members within the community. Four open-ended questions addressed feelings of a sense of community in each community by exploring why participants joined, whether they felt the community had a strong sense of community, whether sense of community was important within the community, and how participants judged sense of community in other, similar communities.

Results

Measuring Sense of Community

Internal consistency for the BSCS scale was high for responses in guild (Cronbach's a = 0.94), neighborhood (Cronbach's a = 0.95), online community (Cronbach's a = 0.86), and community of choice (Cronbach's a = 0.94). The alphas for guild, neighborhood, and community of choice may have been high enough to suggest repetitive questions. The four subscales in the BSCS were reliable for guild (r ranged from .56 to .89), neighborhood (r ranged from .73 to .91), and community of choice (r ranged from .55 to .79). Three of the four subscales were reliable in online community (r ranged from .58 to .86), but Influence was not, with r = .08. Although it was reliable in the other communities, Influence was consistently the lowest subscale across all identified communities.

Community BSCS scores were calculated by taking the mean of the aggregate responses for each community, with a score of 1 being the lowest sense of community and 5 the highest possible sense of community. Guild (3.9) and community of choice (4.1) had the highest BSCS scores. These two scores did not significantly differ from one another, but both scores were significantly higher than online community's BSCS score of 3.4 (with $t(62) = 4.59$, $p < .001$ for guild and $t(51) = 4.53$, $p < .001$ for community of choice) and neighborhood's BSCS score of 2.7 (with $t(71) = 8.73$, $p < .001$ for guild, and $t(57) = 8.46$, $p < .001$ for community of choice). The online community BSCS score of 3.4 was also significantly higher than the neighborhood score of 2.7, with $t(62) = 5.75, p < .001$.

Demographic data were explored as predictors of sense of community mean scores for each of the four communities using stepwise multiple regression. The most common response for each variable was used as the reference category and categorical variables were dummy-coded for use in regression models. All variables were screened for outliers, missing values, normality, skewness, kurtosis, and linearity. The first model variable to significantly predict BSCS scores was the method of contact with other community members. Although method of contact was a significant predictor across communities, the actual method of contact predicting sense of community score for guild (in-game chat), online community (chat or a forum), and neighborhood (in-person contact) was different. The participant's answer for overall sense of community score was also significant in models predicting BSCS scores in guild and neighborhood.

Regression results showed that a seven-variable model significantly predicted BSCS scores for guild, $R^2 = .70$, $R^2 adj = .67$, $F(7,60) = 20.10$, $p < .001$, and accounted for 70.1% of variance in its mean score. The top predictors were in-game chat, years online, and overall sense of community. A two-variable model including method of contact with other members and ethnicity significantly predicted BSCS scores for online community, $R^2 = .18$, $R^2 adj = .15$, $F(2,47) = 5.31$, $p = .01$, and accounted for 18.4% of variance in its mean score. Regression results showed that a four-variable model significantly predicted BSCS scores for neighborhood, $R^2 = .40$, $R^2 adj = .37$, $F(4,65) = 10.90$, $p < .001$, and accounted for 40.1% of variance in its mean score. The top predictors were in-person contact and overall sense of community. Regression results showed that a two-variable model including invitation method and education level significantly predicted BSCS scores for community of choice, $R^2 = .47$, $R^2 adj = .45$, $F(2,49) = 21.97$, $p < .001$, and accounted for 47.3% of variance in the mean score.

Characterizing Sense of Community

Text analysis showed that 76% of open responses describing what sense of community meant fell within the categories of Membership and Shared Emotional Connection. Categories for text analysis were identified with

Leximancer by analyzing answers to the question "Please explain the phrase 'sense of community'" using default settings in the software, which automatically identified concepts and larger themes using a thesaurus. The themes identified by Leximancer were reviewed in relation to seven categories identified in the sense of community literature. Most concepts identified in the responses fit the traditional four factors Shared Emotional Connection, Membership, Influence, and Integration and Fulfillment of Needs. However, the additional factor Friendship was included in final categorization. In addition to being identified in the exploratory analysis as an emergent concept, past literature supports Friendship as a separate factor rather than grouping it with relationships and bonds under Shared Emotional Connection (Blanchard & Markus, 2004). The Coding Analysis Toolkit (CAT) was used to assign categories to individual responses. A single response could be assigned multiple categories, as in the example "You feel like you belong there. You have similar goals, experiences, and ideas about how things should be done." This response was coded for both Shared Emotional Connection and Membership. See Table 1 for details on factors used to describe sense of community in open responses.

Table 1

Factors Identified in Comments About Sense of Community

General SoC[a]	Membership		SEM[b]		IFN[c]		Influence		Friendship	
	F	%	F	%	F	%	F	%	F	%
All	47	41	40	35	12	11	5	4	10	9
SoC Importance[d]	Membership		SEM		IFN		Influence		Friendship	
	F	%	F	%	F	%	F	%	F	%
Guild	13	15	40	48	20	24	5	6	6	7
Neighborhood	1	5	5	24	12	57	1	5	2	9
Online Community	5	9	31	59	2	4	1	2	14	26
Community of Choice	7	14	21	42	11	22	2	4	1	2
Total	26	11	97	40	45	19	9	4	23	10
SoC Presence[e]	Membership		SEM[a]		IFN[b]		Influence		Friendship	
	F	%	F	%	F	%	F	%	F	%
Guild	4	5	45	59	21	27	1	1	0	0
Neighborhood	2	3	41	63	7	11	10	15	3	5
Online Community	5	9	31	57	2	4	1	2	1	2
Community of Choice	7	14	21	42	11	22	2	4	1	2
Total	18	7	138	56	41	17	14	6	5	2

a. Question: Please explain the phrase "Sense of Community."
b. Shared Emotional Connection
c. Integration and Fulfillment of Needs
d. Question: Is sense of community important in your guild (community/neighborhood)? Why or why not?
e. Question: How can you tell if another guild (community/neighborhood) has a sense of community?

Neighborhoods were the only community in which the majority of participants did not feel that sense of community was important, with 52% saying it was not important to the community. On the opposite end, 87% of participants said sense of community was important in their guild.

Responses to open-ended questions were explored within each community and showed that three of the four traditional factors (Shared Emotional Connection, Membership, and Integration and Fulfillment of Needs) were common factors used to describe both the importance and strength of sense of community across all community types. See Table 1 for details on factors used to describe sense of community in open responses. There was a significant difference between which factor was most cited in guilds and neighborhoods (F(3,204) = 2.95, $p < .05$, $\eta^2 = .042$) with Integration and Fulfillment of Needs most referenced in neighborhood and Shared Emotional Connection most mentioned in guild. Across all four communities, participants identified Shared Emotional Connection as the top factor used to identify sense of community in a similar community. However, in online communities the top response was Not Possible, outranking any of the factors.

Text analysis was also applied to explore the meaning of "online community" to participants by categorizing the communities participants identified as the online community to which they belonged. The survey itself did not provide any examples of online communities. In the text analysis, categories were mainly built around Leximancer themes identified from the responses but also loosely categorized around the most common online communities to which Americans belong (Pierce & Boekelheide, 2009; USC Annenberg School for Communication, 2008). The categories that emerged fit into two classifications: online community formats (social news, social network, forum, funding platform, chat, video site, and image site) and online community purposes (social, game, special interest, hobby, and social cause).

Conclusions

Results indicate that the BSCS can be used to measure the four factors of sense of community in online communities. Additionally, participants characterized sense of community in both online and offline communities using the traditional four factors from sense of community theory. The similarities across community types in how we characterize sense of community and what predicts BSCS scores suggest that use of sense of community theory and traditional scales can help us to understand communities even as they evolve to use new technologies and overlap places and spaces. Application of a standard scale can enable future research to compare diverse communities.

Connections

That members were contacting one another in some way that was enabled by the community was the top predictor of sense of community score in three of the four communities. The connections, ranging from in-game chat to in-person contact, varied by community. The best way to connect with a specific community may be based on the goals of that community. For instance, the gaming guilds were focused on working together as a team, and their ability to plan and carry out group activities was enabled by in-game chat. Despite the specific selection of in-game chat, this predictor would likely be as strong if technology evolved and guilds were able to use video chat or virtual reality to enable that connection. At the core, the ability to connect with other members in a community is a predictor of the sense of community within it. With poor or limited contact, factors of sense of community would be more difficult to develop among members.

Additionally, participants' overall sense of community score was a predictor of higher sense of community scores within both guild and neighborhood. This could be a sign of the "rich-get-richer" theory (Kraut et al., 2002), which has been applied to online interactions, showing that people who have more friends offline are likely to have more friends online also. In the case of sense of community, someone who already feels an overall strong sense of community across his/her life may be better able to find or build similar strong connections in communities regardless of their online or offline nature.

Results also showed that the strength of sense of community varies across online communities. Differences between online communities as well as differences between online and offline connections are an important area for future research. Many things beyond the online format could be impacting the strength of sense of community. Going back to the ability of members to connect within a community, online communities with similar intentions and reach could see different levels of sense of community based on whether or not they provide an easy-to-use method of contacting and connecting with other members. For communities with managers aiming to improve the sense of community, making sure members are comfortable with using the main communication method could be an important step towards a more engaged community. As our communities evolve with technology, the options shift rapidly. As the results show, no two community types used the same method of connecting, but in all cases the connection was a predictor of the sense of community score.

Just as online communities have not often been compared to one another, communities with the same aim existing online and offline have only recently begun to be included together in sense of community studies. The next step for research is to look deeper at how communities compare to one another. Identifying similarities and differences may lead to an understanding of what enables one community to flourish while another falls short of its goal. Don Grant did an excellent job of focusing in on this topic in his paper *Using Social Media for Sobriety Recovery? Beliefs, Behaviors, and Surprises from Users of Face-to-Face and Social Media Sobriety Support*. Understanding how online social support compares to offline social support, and whether a mixture of online and offline support can benefit members, will enable communities to focus on what connects members in addition to what communities can offer to their members.

Digital Etiquette and Security

Perhaps one of the most interesting findings from this study was not one that was intentionally measured or one that can be quantified, but something that is deeply rooted in digital citizenship. As an outsider entering the online gaming community, the primary researcher made a point of playing the game for three months and interacting with other players during that time to learn not only the game interface but also the cultural norms. Additionally, the research assistant was recruited for her experience in the game. However, the in-game attempts to collect survey data were met with suspicion. Both the primary researcher and the research assistant were banned as spammers within the first day of attempting to invite participants to the survey.

Although this was a setback that required more time and effort to acquire participants, it also showed a deep connection among the players that was mirrored in the high BSCS guild score. This protectiveness of other players goes beyond the guild and shows a sense of community within the game as a whole. Rather than simply ignoring messages and chats with invitations to participate in the research, players reported them. There is an overall connection among players, and a desire to keep the entire community safe from possible risk rather than simply looking out for oneself. The researchers were an outside force with the potential to cause harm, and they were treated as such.

Sense of Community Factors

How well an online community addresses the Shared Emotional Connection of members may also play a role in the potential it has to build a strong sense of community among members. Although participants mentioned all four of the traditional sense of community factors in open-ended responses, some were more prevalent than others. Shared Emotional Connection was the highest-ranking factor identified in the importance of sense of community within guild and online community, in contrast with neighborhood, where Integration and Fulfillment of Needs was the top factor. Shared Emotional Connection was also the most cited factor to look for to determine whether another community had a sense of community when observing it from the outside. The concepts that make up Shared Emotional Connection include members: sharing a history; spending time together; investing in the community; and forming relationships. The prevalence of this factor was especially interesting in online communities, because they have often been thought of as spaces where we interact around a shared interest or goal but do not build strong relationships. However, the emotional connections built between members were cited as important more often than the ability to achieve community-related goals. For community managers, this may mean that providing information and opportunities can be more meaningful to members if they also have the ability to share these factors in a way that builds relationships and requires investment of members' time, money, or intimacy.

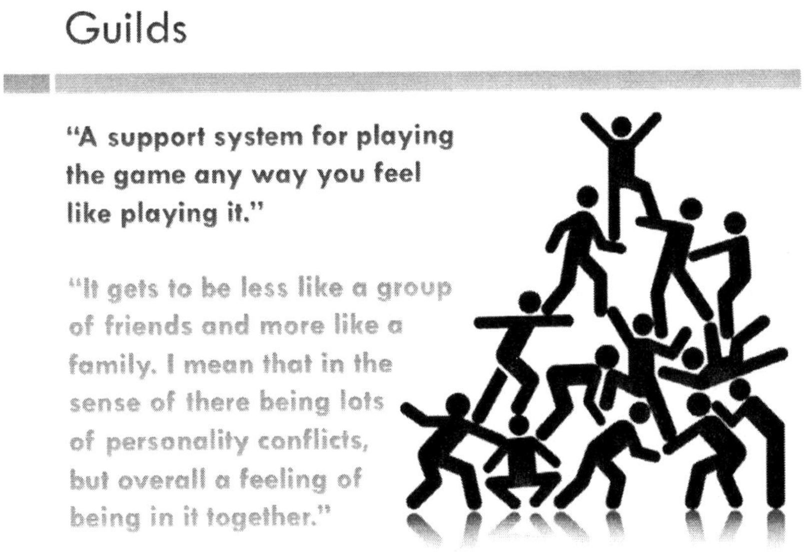

Guilds

"A support system for playing the game any way you feel like playing it."

"It gets to be less like a group of friends and more like a family. I mean that in the sense of there being lots of personality conflicts, but overall a feeling of being in it together."

Figure 1. Participant comments about sense of community within guilds

Online Communities

"Membership is purely about
your own involvement and
whether or not you choose
to be a part of it."

**"You know you've
become a part of the
community when people
reply to your posts and
show genuine interest in
what you have to say."**

Figure 2. Participant comments about sense of community within online communities

Friendship was the second highest factor mentioned in the importance of sense of community for online communities, which were distinct from all other communities. Although Shared Emotional Connection does include relationships and bonds among members, the concentration is on experiences within the community itself. The concepts underlying Friendship differ by emphasizing a relationship that goes beyond community interactions. The most common purpose participants in this study identified for the online community was being social. Additionally, 37% stated they had joined the online community because of an existing friendship. Our use of social networks has evolved from connecting with strangers over shared interests, when fewer people had access to the Internet, to reconnecting with old friends, relatives, classmates, and co-workers today. Although the purposes for using social sites are broad, this study asked specifically about sense of community within the online community, thus identifying that the results are similar to other studies that look at communities within social networks rather than studying social networks on their own (Reich, 2010). This emphasis on friendships outside of the community, formed before or after membership began, may be unique to social online communities.

In past research, it has been noted that online communities showed lower levels of Influence than traditional communities (Blanchard & Markus, 2004). Concepts such as conformity, the community's influencing members, members making a difference in the group, and mattering define the Influence factor. It was thought that online communities had less impact on members' real lives, accounting for the lower levels of Influence. However, in the current study Influence was the least mentioned traditional factor across all communities. Where Influence showed up the most was in the local neighborhood, but rather than indicating a positive community experience that was missing from online interactions, the comments involving Influence and neighborhood were mostly negative. Participants mentioned unfavorable forms of control such as bossy neighbors and too many signs outlining the neighborhood rules. Interestingly, participants also mentioned Influence in a more positive manner when it was used to identify sense of community in other neighborhoods. In those comments tidy yards, cleanliness, and consistent appearances took on a more favorable note than what was seen as oppressive in their own neighborhood. In contrast to negative personal experiences with Influence, the items in this study were all positively worded and open-ended questions asked about the strength and importance of a sense of community. The conflicting viewpoints on Influence could explain its absence in the responses. Additionally, the Influence subscale in the BSCS had the lowest reliability score across all communities. It is possible that Influence, while important, is not seen as a positive aspect of community and is thus under-reported in sense of community research.

Neighborhoods

"Our neighborhood
has 50 signs declaring
what is NOT to be
done on grounds."

"I don't see any special reason to connect with
people who happen to live in the same area as me
because they live near me."

Figure 3. Participant comments about sense of community within neighborhoods

Rethinking Online Communities

In this study, participants were asked to self-identify two communities
and answer questions about the sense of community within those communities. One question asked participants to identify an "online community," the other simply asked for a community but did not rule out online
communities. Most participants named social sites and social media (e.g.,
Facebook, Reddit) when they identified an online community. The sense
of community in these communities was higher than that of local neighborhoods, but lower than both online guilds and the other self-identified
communities. Responses for the other self-identified community were not
only mixed in terms of the purpose of the community but also in terms
of whether the community connected online. However, despite the community of choice crossing online/offline connections there was little overlap with those communities identified as an "online community." For the
most part, social sites and social media platforms were not included in the
community of choice. Only when "online" was included did a limitation
to what communities were identified seem to appear. This same limitation is almost instantaneous in any discussion if someone brings up online

communities. It is as though we have been trained to think of high-profile social media companies as the necessary and default "online" communities, which we expect to fulfill our social and communal needs. Instead, though, the breadth of connections available in social networks can become burdensome and the platforms themselves do not offer a strong sense of community. However, past research has found that while social media platforms do not fulfill the criteria for being defined as communities, groups can form within social media that are communities, using the tools provided by the platforms for quick and easy connections (Reich, 2010). While participants in this study identified platforms such as Facebook and Reddit as "online communities," those smaller groups within the social platforms were some of the communities identified in the community of choice. These communities breached the online/offline divide and were ranked as having a higher sense of community than purely online communities.

One such community identified is the professional group. These groups exchanged support online, focused on everyday business needs, and were included in the community of choice question but not in the online community question. They are still digitally supported and often connect within a social media platform, but perhaps it is the link to "real life" that makes them something other than "online communities" in how they are defined. Another high-ranking community of choice identified in this study was the gaming group. Both online and in-person groups were listed as communities and came with a high overall sense of community.

The term "online communities" is in need of a reboot. At best, in popular usage, the term brings Facebook to mind. At worst it can bring up insular groups feeding closed-minded ideas. In reality, online communities can exist not only online, and not necessarily separate from reality, but also offline and in between the two spaces. Whether friends join an online community to stay in touch or guild members seek one another out in person after gaming together, our community connections are fluid. Technological tools can support community connections, no matter the origin of the community. By aiming to understand how we define communities, how we connect within communities, and what elements help communities to foster a strong sense of community, we can enable research to benefit practice. By applying these concepts to build meaningful communities—connected both online and offline—we can increase the reach of communities and their support of life satisfaction, efficacy, and mental and physical health.

We are at a point where digital interactions are noticeably impacting our everyday lives. As with any community, in addition to the positive outcomes of a strong sense of community being built through digital connections, there can also be negative outcomes. Whether these manifest as international-scale social shaming on social media or local bullying carried out in online spaces, the impact is real in both the digital and physical spaces. By understanding the factors that are strongest in an online community's sense of community, we can begin to see whether there are differences among the positive and negative community outcomes as well. As we all struggle with the balance between our power to reach anyone anywhere in just four degrees of separation and our responsibilities to our local and online communities, it can do us good to remember that we are all members of multiple communities and what we do online impacts the real lives of everyone involved. Our behavior, our digital citizenship, is part of our membership not only in communities of interest and local neighborhoods but in our wider society that is now online, offline, and in between.

Limitations

The sample size of this study is small due in part to the protective nature of the gaming community and in part to the length of the survey. Most participants were recruited from outside the game, with very few of the guild members who were invited directly taking part. Additionally, participant comments on the survey length suggest that future studies may find more success comparing only two communities rather than four in order to reduce the time investment by participants.

Future Research

Each community is unique, but the ties that bind members together are founded on factors similar to other communities. Measuring the traditional factors of sense of community across communities and exploring how members experience community within them can provide an understanding of what factors are most important in different community types. Additionally, looking at how the communities support member connections with one another may shed some light on how to build more effective communities in the future. How we experience that sense of community online is similar to community experiences based in physical spaces. Yet there is still a need to explore the differences between online and offline support from similar communities and between varying online communities. Additionally, the Influence factor's negative interpretation might be investigated, especially in regard to potential underreporting.

References

Anderson, M. R. (2010). Community psychology, political efficacy, and trust. *Political Psychology, 31*(1), 59-84. Retrieved March 1, 2010, from Wiley InterScience.

Backstrom, L., Boldi, P., Rosa, M., Ugander, J., & Vigna, S. (2012). Four Degrees of Separation [Electronic version]. *arXiv, Computer Science,* http://arxiv.org/abs/1111.4570.

Blanchard, A. L., & Markus, M. L. (2004). The experienced "sense" of a virtual community: Characteristics and processes. *The DATA BASE for Advances in Information Systems, 35*(1), 64-71. Retrieved January 27, 2011, from Google Scholar.

Brodsky, A. E., Loomis, C., & Marx, C. M. (2002). Expanding the conceptualisation of PSOC. In A. T. Fisher, C. C. Sonn, & B. J. Bishop (Eds.), *Psychological sense of community: Research, applications, and implications* (pp. 319-336). New York, NY: Kluwer Academic/Plenum.

Chavis, D. M., & Pretty, G.M.H. (1999). Sense of community: Advances in measurement and application. *Journal of Community Psychol-*

ogy, 27(6), 635-642. Retrieved August 24, 2008, from Wiley InterScience.

Hampton, K. (2001). *Living the wired life in the wired suburbs: Netville, globalization and civic society.* (dissertation). Retrieved from Dissertations & Theses: Full Text database.

Hoffman, P. R. (2008). *"But are we really friends?": Online social networking and community in undergraduate students.* (Dissertation). Retrieved from FirstSearch.

Kraut, R., Kiesler, S., Boneva, B., Cummings, J., Helgeson, V., & Crawford, A. (2002). Internet paradox revisited. *Journal of Social Issues, 58*(1), 49-74. Retrieved January 9, 2011, from http://kraut. hciresearch.org/sites/kraut.hciresearch.org/files/articles/kraut02-paradox-revisited-16-20-2.pdf.

McMillan, D. W., & Chavis, D. M. (1986). Sense of community: A definition and theory. *Journal of Community Psychology, 14,* 6-23. Retrieved July 8, 2008, from Google Scholar.

Obst, P., & Starfurik, J. (2010). Online we are all able bodied: Online psychological sense of community and social support found through membership of disability-specific websites promotes well-being for people living with a physical disability. *Journal of Community & Applied Social Psychology, 20*(6), 525-531. Retrieved February 9, 2011, from Wiley Online Library.

Obst, P., Zinkiewicz, L., & Smith, S. G. (2002). Sense of community in science fiction fandom, Part 1: Understanding sense of community in an international community of interest. *Journal of Community Psychology, 30*(1), 87-103. Retrieved July 12, 2008, from Wiley InterScience.

Peterson, N. A., Speer, P. W., & McMillan, D. W. (2008). Validation of a Brief Sense of Community Scale: Confirmation of the principal theory of sense of community. *Journal of Community Psychology, 36*(1), 61-73. Retrieved August 24, 2008, from Wiley InterScience.

Pierce, J., & Boekelheide, A. (2009). *Highlights: The 2009 Digital Fu-*

ture Project—Year eight. [Press Release]. Los Angeles, CA: USC Annenberg School for Communication. Retrieved August 16, 2009, from http://www.digitalcenter.org/pages/site_content.asp?intGlobalId=20.

Prezza, M., Amici, M., Roberti, T., & Tedeschi, G. (2001). Sense of community referred to the whole town: Its relations with neighboring, loneliness, life satisfaction, and area of residence. *Journal of Community Psychology, 29*(1), 29-52. Retrieved May 1, 2010, from Wiley InterScience.

Prohn, S. M. (2009). *Interest group psychological sense of community: Measurement and the monolithic fallacy.* (Master's Thesis). Retrieved from FirstSearch.

Reich, S. M. (2010). Adolescents' sense of community on MySpace and Facebook: A mixed-methods approach. *Journal of Community Psychology, 38*(6), 688-705. Retrieved October 6, 2010, from Wiley Online Library.

Roberts, L. D., Smith, L. M., & Pollock, C. (2002). MOOing till the cows come home: The search for sense of community in virtual environments. In A. T. Fisher, C. C. Sonn, & B. J. Bishop (Eds.), *Psychological sense of community: Research, applications, and implications* (pp. 223-245). New York, NY: Kluwer Academic/ Plenum.

Shinn, M., & Toohey, S. M. (2002). Community contexts of human welfare. *Annual Review of Psychology, 54*, 427-459. Retrieved July 5, 2008, from Annual Reviews.

USC Annenberg School for Communication. (2008). *Highlights: The 2008 Digital Future Project—Year seven.* [Press Release]. Los Angeles, CA: USC Annenberg School for Communication. Retrieved August 16, 2009, from http://www.digitalcenter.org/pages/site_content.asp?intGlobalId=20.

About the Author

Jenny Fremlin, PhD, works and plays in Southeast Alaska, where she explores mindful media and how we can support local community with online connections. She is an active member of numerous local boards, including government and nonprofit organizations, and active in national and international psychological organizations. Dr. Fremlin's media background spans more than two decades, with roles in print and digital design, photography, creative direction, magazine management, mobile app development, business consulting, student advising, and personalized training aimed at making all of these data and technology evolutions accessible. When she's not applying the study of media psychology to practice, she can be found hiking in the rain forest. Her website is jennyfremlin.com.

ADOLESCENTS' META-PERSPECTIVES OF
MEDIA IMMERSION

Yashica Holmes-Smith, PhD, Fielding Graduate University, USA

Abstract: A study was conducted to explore the views of teens who demonstrated heavy media use. Media tracking sheets were distributed to adolescents between the ages of 13 and 19 years. Twelve of the heaviest media users were selected to participate in a qualitative study of their views about heavy media use. Participants were asked to maintain a media journal for two weeks and to participate in an interview about media use and the perceived impact of heavy media use. Eight participants submitted journals and completed interviews. Categorical content analyses were conducted to analyze data collected from selection sheets, journal entries, and interview transcripts. Themes were identified to offer insight into adolescents' experiences with media and the influence of heavy media on adolescents' academic, social, and personal well-being. The identified themes provided insight into the teens' perspectives on media and its influence on relationships, time management, their individuality, and their behavior. In addition, teens reported a rise in media literacy and stated that they gained awareness about their media use when asked to monitor and reflect on their media practices.

Keywords: adolescents, teens, media

Introduction

Adolescents and young adults are among the highest consumers of media (Rideout, Foehr, & Roberts, 2010; Generations, 2010). According to reports from the AAP Committee on Public Education and the Council on Communications and Media (AAP, n.d.), adults often express concerns about the effects of media on teens' attitudes and behaviors. While it is important to research and manage the risks associated with heavy media use, it is also important to consider and maximize the benefits of balanced media and technology use. The AAP article stated that the risks and concerns about media use included displaced time, distraction from healthy activities (e.g., physical activity, studying), poor grades, risks to physical health (i.e., less physical activity, poor eating habits, distorted body image as a result of time spent using media and exposure to media messages about food and beauty), negative effects on social well-being as a result of time taken from face-to-face relationships, negative effects on emotional well-being (i.e., depression, poor personal contentment), exposure to messages that negatively shape attitudes and behaviors, exposure to violence and aggression, uninhibited online behaviors and harassment (i.e., cyberbullying), social learning and imitation of negative behaviors witnessed in media, exposure to sexual content and content that normalizes risky behaviors, sexting, online sexual solicitation, exposure to ads and content promoting substance use (i.e., tobacco, alcohol, prescription drugs), exposure to content that promotes stereotypes, negative feedback (i.e., hurtful comments from others), and privacy risks and violations.

The same article stated that healthy media use offers a number of benefits by providing access to the following: learning opportunities and academic activities; health information; expressive and therapeutic activities; and creative activities. In addition it offers opportunities to pursue the following: identity exploration; socialization; connecting with others with similar interests; extending face-to-face relationships; involvement in community projects and organizations; seeking social support; finding platforms for shy individuals to be more open and social; and entertainment and distraction from negative realities (Dominick, 1996, as cited in Roberts, Henriksen, & Foehr, 2004).

It is possible that gaining insight into teens' views of their media world can help adults promote positive media practices and reduce the risks associated with unhealthy media habits. The purpose of this study is to qualitatively explore the role of media from adolescents' perspectives. The research evaluated teens' perceptions of their media experiences along with the positive and negative factors they associate with their media habits. The study qualitatively gathered and explored data about teens' media practices, experiences, interpretations, and positive and negative outcomes as they relate to personal, social, and academic well-being. While each teen's situation and perspective is subjective, the findings of the study can offer overall insights into teens' experiences of heavy media use. Such insights can be used to guide adults' discussions with adolescents and to promote critical thinking about media use among adolescents.

Methodology and Project Description

Media tracking sheets were used as selection tools. Participants were asked to record the media platforms they used and the amount of time they spent using each form of media across a period of two days. Participants who reported at least 16 hours of media use per day were categorized as heavy media users and selected to participate in the qualitative portion of the study. The selected teens were asked to keep a media tracking journal for two weeks. Tracking sheets and journaling instructions asked participants to record the times of day they used media, the types of media they used, where they were, who they were with, other activities they were involved in at the same time, and their thoughts and appraisal of their media experience. They were then asked to participate in an interview about their journal reports and experiences.

RobbGrieco and Hobbs (2012) discussed the role of facilitating active reasoning in helping students to develop analytical and critical thinking skills. The current study facilitated active reasoning, as the researcher followed up on many of the participants' initial responses to interview questions. In addition, the tracking and journaling activities helped participants to reflect on their daily use of media. The content of the journal entries and interview transcripts was analyzed using an open coding and constant comparative methods.

Findings

The study included responses from eight teens (age 13–19) who were exposed to at least 16 hours of media per day. Of the eight participants, seven were female and one was male. Seven of the participants were African

American and one was Caucasian. Data about each teen's media use were collected from each of the eight participants' media tracking sheets, journals, and interviews.

Participants' names, ages, and average hours of media use can be seen in Figure 1.

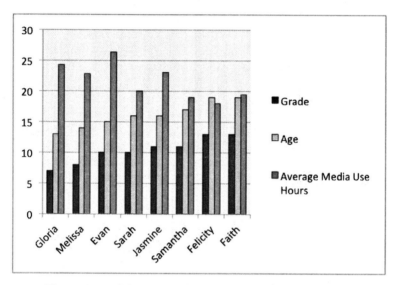

Figure 1. Participants' grades, ages, and average media use

The study included: Gloria, a 13-year-old Black female in seventh grade; Melissa, a 14-year-old White female in eighth grade; Evan, a 15-year-old Black male in tenth grade; Sarah, a 16-year-old Black female in tenth grade; Jasmine, a 16-year-old Black female in 11th grade; Samantha, a 17-year-old Black female in 11th grade; Felicity, a 19-year-old Black female completing her first year of college; and Faith, a 19-year-old Black female completing her first year of college.

Overall, participants used more media during the weekend than they did during weekdays. Participants averaged 23 hours and 21 minutes of weekend use and 19 hours and 57 minutes of weekday use. The most heavily used platforms for both weekend and weekdays included cell phones, music, and television, respectively. The least used platforms included print and movie theater. Participants did not report any instances of accessing printed media during weekdays, and they reported attending movie theaters during weekends only. The average amount of media use ranged from 18 hours to 26 hours and 28 minutes. Participants between the ages of 13 and 16 averaged 20 hours or more of media use. Participants between the ages of 17 and 19 averaged less than 20 hours of media use. The male participant reported the highest amount of media exposure. He averaged 26 hours and 28 minutes of media exposure.

Content analysis of transcribed interviews revealed a number of themes and subthemes. These themes represented topics and ideas that were repeatedly expressed across participants. They summarized factors that were included in each of the adolescents' responses about experiences with media. The following themes were identified:

- Using Media for Good
- Media as a Double-Edged Sword
- Mediated Relationships: Connecting and Disconnecting
- A Matter of Time: Time Saved and Time Displaced
- My Media, My Self: Self and Individuality
- Entertainment and Distraction
- Above the Influence
- Media Literacy on the Rise
- Gaining Awareness Through Monitoring and Reflection

Using Media for Good

Participants discussed the benefits and positive uses of media, such as using media for learning, motivation, and to help themselves and others. One of the most common factors included using media to improve academic performance. The participants talked about the ways in which their use of media helped them to complete assignments, access helpful information, and ultimately to improve their grades. For example, Melissa stated:

If I'm ever confused on anything, like in algebra, I'll go on YouTube and look up an instructional video with the professors teaching me how to do it. If I don't understand, it helps me understand things better in my classes.

Similarly, Sarah stated, "If I'm answering a problem in school and I really don't know how to do it, I can use Google to help me with it." Gloria added, "I just made the honor roll and I believe the iPad has helped me a lot because I can find out more information about different things." Gloria reported that her school provided an iPad for every student. She discussed the helpfulness of using the device to access the school's grading system, which allowed her to monitor her grades and to use them as a guide. She stated that having constant access to her grades and progress reports let her know which areas she needed to focus on and improve in. Faith, a first-year college student, discussed the ways in which her media use helped her to coordinate study groups.

In addition to discussing media use as it related to academic performance, participants talked about the role of media in helping them to prepare for future careers. For example, Gloria aspires to become a real estate broker. She talked about a show called *Love It or List It* and explained that the show focused on renovating and selling houses. Gloria explained that some of the television shows she watched offered career guidance. Along the same lines, Jasmine stated that she was interested in premed and used the Internet to look up information about diseases and finding cures. Felicity stated she wanted to become a teacher, and used media to learn more about how technology can be used in the field of education because "technology is heavily used in the school systems."

In addition to using media for academic and career guidance, participants talked about using media to regulate their own emotions and to motivate themselves. For example, Faith stated, "I listen to music and it makes me happy." Felicity said, "I can get on Vine or Instagram and see a funny post or funny video and it can kind of make me smile or laugh if I'm not in a good mood or something like that." Similarly, Jasmine stated she listened to inspirational gospel music to help her to get through her day. Samantha reported using media to seek social support to help her cope with emotional ups and downs. Jasmine and Faith reported how they used media to help them to improve and maintain their physical health. Jasmine said:

I'm trying to lose weight. I found that going on YouTube videos and looking at people's strength photos helps motivate me to keep going and helps me to lose weight. I enjoy getting on the computer and going to YouTube and looking at people to see how they lost the weight. It gives me motivation that I can do it, too.

Faith stated, "I stay physically fit. I use my phone as a timer, so you can do sessions and reps and all that. And the Wii has yoga, and they've got a little balance beam."

Some participants reported being good digital citizens by using media to help others to feel good. Melissa discussed the ways in which she used social media to express positive feelings toward others. She stated:

Yesterday was my sister's birthday and I posted a picture of me and her and a long paragraph about how much I appreciate her and all that she does for me; and how I love her and she'll always have a place in my heart. She commented back and said, "I love you so much" and put a little kissy face. I think that made her day.

Another participant, Evan, discussed how he was able to use his personal cell phone to help his uncle keep an important medical appointment that saved his uncle's life. He explained how his uncle's telephone number had changed and medical representatives were unable to reach him. Evan was listed as a relative and he was able to act as a liaison to make sure his uncle received the medical information and services he needed.

Some of the other positive uses discussed included using media to engage in creative activities, to capture special moments with family and friends, and to play an active role in community organizations or churches. Melissa reported playing an important role in her church's service production. She reported operating computer equipment to project song lyrics and using a video camera to record the church service. Melissa also discussed using computers to make creative PowerPoint presentations and to get creative ideas from websites such as Pinterest.com. She stated, "I think using computers allows me to be more creative." Evan discussed capturing special moments with his family using his camera and video recorder. The participants' statements demonstrate how they use media to cope, to seek social support, to better themselves, and to help others. All of the aforementioned examples illustrate the ways in which media can be used for positive purposes.

Media as a Double-Edged Sword

All of the participants stated that media and technology were both good and bad. Each of them discussed ways in which media helped and hindered them in various areas. Participants talked about the pros and cons of media as it related to academic performance, social relationships, and health. While participants talked about the positive and negative aspects of media throughout their interviews, this section will highlight statements in which participants acknowledged their contrasting views of media simultaneously. For example, Jasmine, who talked about using YouTube to help motivate herself to reach her weight loss goals, stated:

> It helps and it hinders. It helps that I can go on there and look at people do it, like lose weight or whatever, but it hinders because there are times when I know I should be exercising but I'm so glued to the media—I mean glued to the television or glued to my telephone—that I don't get up and go to the gym.

Nearly all of the participants talked about the ways in which media helped them academically, but also distracted them from academic assignments at times. To illustrate the double-sided nature of media immersion, many of the participants used phases such as, "I would say it's 50/50" (Evan), "It kind of helps, but then again, it doesn't" (Felicity), and "there could be ups and downs with society and media" (Melissa). Melissa talked about gaining and losing friends via media. She stated:

> Just be careful what you're doing, because you can gain or lose friends with media. You can hurt people's feelings really easily, but you also can boost people's confidence and you can be nice to people. It just all depends on how you conduct yourself when you are using media.

Likewise, while talking about relationships, Faith said, "It can make the best of it or the worst. It just depends on the people, not actually the media." In regard to academic performance, Felicity said:

It can be a negative, it can be a positive, because they can use it for the good as far as being up on today's current events. And then it can be very negative to where they lose focus; they're stuck on media and not staying focused.

Similarly, when asked about the impact of media, Evan said, "I would say 50/50, because it sometimes gets you in trouble, and it's sometimes a helpful way to improve grades and improve your academics."

All of the students testified to the helpful and unhelpful nature of using media. They all discussed the positive and negative effects of media on some aspect of their lives or on society as a whole. In addition to providing a range of examples to demonstrate how media was both good and bad in various ways, they all provided statements that to some degree said the impact of media use depended on the person using media, and not the media itself. They all seemed to agree that media and technology were neutral, and that it was up to individuals to make media experiences good or bad. The participants took the blame off media and placed the responsibility on individuals.

Mediated Relationships: Connecting and Disconnecting

Along the same lines of media being a double-edged sword, all of the participants talked about the ways media helped and hurt social relationships. In this section, I will talk about the effects of media on relationships and the ways in which participants believe media connects and disconnects. While the "double-edged sword" section highlighted pros and cons that were expressed simultaneously, this section will discuss views (about media connecting and disconnecting relationships) that were expressed separately.

Connecting

All of the participants reported using media to connect with friends and family, particularly relatives they could not see face-to-face on a regular basis. Media was reportedly used to connect people in long distance relationships and to coordinate face-to-face meetings. Participants reported using media to meet new people and to connect with people who shared similar interests. The participants talked about ways media and technology could be used to build or enhance face-to-face relationships, to connect with people who live far away, to reunite with people they hadn't corresponded with in a long time, and to meet new people. Gloria discussed using television programs to bring families together. She stated, "If the whole family has a special TV show that they watch together on a special day, then it could bring the whole family together." Melissa also talked about connecting with her family. Participants discussed the ways family members used media to receive and to provide social support.

Many of the participants talked about using media to keep in touch with friends from school over the summer, and to keep in touch with friends who live far away. Jasmine talked about the fact that she and her family moved to their current location two years ago. She explained that she missed her old friends and it was hard finding new friends after she relocated. She used media to keep in contact with friends from her previous location, and maintaining old friendships was helpful for her. Similarly, Melissa reported using media to stay in touch with some of her best friends who lived in another state. She stated that media was good for their social lives because it allowed them to keep in contact and to plan visits. Faith talked about the role media has had in her social life as she discussed reuniting with a long-lost friend. Faith stated, "Recently, I've connected with a friend I haven't talked to since middle school. We met at the Youth Summit and now we're reconnected after seven years. Thus, I think media has a real big impact on my social life." Evan said media helped him to explore and find new friendships. When asked about the role of media in friendships, he said, "It really helps you build relationships among your friends and you have stronger feelings toward your friends." Along those same lines, Melissa said she has gotten to know a lot of her friends through texting and phone conversations. She said:

> I meet them in person, then I get their number, and then I really get to know them. We're like really close now. Me and my best friend, we met at a ball practice and we exchanged numbers, and now you can

hardly separate us.

These types of statements show how media can be used to build and maintain healthy relationships between family members and friends. This suggests that, when used responsibly, media can play a positive role in the social development of adolescents.

Disconnecting

All of the participants discussed the ways media interfered with the amount of time and attention dedicated to face-to-face relationships and social activities, and they provided examples of instances in which media use caused disconnections between family and friends. Sarah discussed an interesting point about the role of media in her communication with family. She said:

> I talk to my family online, but when they're in my face I don't really talk to them. Because they're right beside me and I'm on my phone talking to other people. But when they're far away, I'll talk to them on the phone or text them and stuff. But if they're in front of me, I'm not going to be in their face talking to them.

Other participants made similar statements and suggested that media was more helpful in connecting relatives who were far away, and often disconnected relatives who lived together or those who saw each other on a regular basis. Participants discussed the role of media in interfering with family time and social support. While most of the participants talked about how their own media habits caused disconnections, a few of them stated that their parents overused media and played a role in the disconnection. For example, Sarah said, "All I do is sit on the phone. And that's how my mom does too, so we just sit on the phone. We don't really have that much communication." Likewise, Melissa said, "My mama just got an iPhone a couple of months ago and that thing has consumed her. Like big time. She is constantly on it." She went on to talk about her mother using her computer and said, "My mama, she'll be on it all the time and I'm like, 'Mama please, just shut the computer. I want to tell you about my day.'" Melissa continued to discuss her family's media use and stated:

When I'm trying to tell them about something I'm struggling with or something I want to tell them about, when they're on the computer, I feel like they're not really paying attention to what I'm saying. They're focused on what they're doing on the phone or computer. When they're doing that on their media device and I'm trying to tell them about a problem I'm having in my life, I feel like they really don't care because they're on their media when I'm trying to tell them something that's wrong with me.

Statements from Melissa and other participants pointed out that adolescents are not the only population immersed in media. Many adults are consumed by media as well. Both teens and adults have contributed to the disconnection facilitated by media immersion. In addition to disconnecting due to lack of attention and time with family members, media has played a role in disconnecting people in other ways. Participants talked about disconnecting from friends as a result of negative comments and arguments facilitated by media. Many of the participants explained that people often say things via media that they would not say face-to-face and, as a result, friendships were sometimes ruined.

A Matter of Time: Time Saved and Time Lost

Participants discussed the concept of media and time in a manner similar to that of media being a double-edged sword. They reported their views about the convenience of using media and the amount of time it saved, but also discussed the amount of time they lost or wasted using media. When asked what they valued about using media, many of the participants said they valued how fast they could communicate or get things done by utilizing technology. For example, Faith discussed the convenience of calling, texting, or using social media as opposed to writing letters and waiting for mail to be physically delivered. She stated:

Now you can just hit somebody up on Facebook or just shoot them a text. It's much easier through text or phone calls and faster than, say, a letter. The quickness of it for the most part is really helpful and resourceful.

Faith said she appreciated the quality and speed of the Wi-Fi connection on her college campus. When asked to elaborate, she said, "You can get what you need right then and there. It's really quick and easy and you don't have to worry about delays or anything getting in your way." Melissa reported:

> I get a lot of my school work done ahead of time, and I don't have to be rushed to try to get things done at the last minute. I have technology at home, so I don't have to do it all at school. So I can get some of my school work done faster.

Participants also talked about the amount of time that can be lost if technology fails. They discussed experiencing delays due to slow Internet connections or Internet crashes. For instance, Faith said the Internet service at her home was not as good because data moved slowly "and it took forever to get anything done." In addition to losing time due to technology issues, all of the participants discussed the concept of displaced time and procrastination. They all stated that the time they spent using media, particularly social media, could have been used to complete more important tasks. For example, Samantha stated:

> I can be doing my work and instead of finishing it I can go to Facebook and spend like two hours, two and a half hours on Facebook and then finish my homework really late, and that causes me to go to bed really late and to be sleepy during school.

Evan also talked about the concept of time as it related to completing school assignments. He reported that he and his friends sometimes called each other to help each other complete assignments quickly, but ended up wasting a lot of time talking and being distracted.

Melissa talked about allowing text messages and calls to interrupt her while completing assignments. She stated, "I think I could get my homework and stuff done a lot faster if I didn't have the cell phone." Melissa also stated, "I can definitely say that when you get on the computer and you start, you look for one thing and you end up staying on there for like two hours straight." While participants valued the amount of time they were able to save using technology for various tasks, they often squandered time by procrastinating and allowing themselves to be distracted while using media.

My Media, My Self: Self and Individuality

Identity development is an important concept for adolescents. Participants in the current study discussed using media to express who they were and to express their individuality. They reported using media to share things about who they were and who they aspired to be. They also used media to engage in and share personal interests. Evan believed his media use defined him as a person, as writing or talking to other people about activities he enjoyed demonstrated what he was personally interested in. When asked how media related to her sense of self, Faith stated, "It allows me to tell the world how unique I am and how I feel about myself. It allows me to express myself in more ways." Gloria said she used her iPad to express how smart she was. Other participants talked about using social media to express their feelings or to post quotes that pertained to them.

Participants discussed media as it related to self-confidence. For example, Melissa stated:

> I think it makes me feel good because, like on Instagram, if I post a picture or something, people will comment and be like, "You're so beautiful!" I feel like it definitely helps me build up self-confidence when people say stuff like that when I post stuff on social media.

According to the participants, social media allows them to state their opinions and to show off their work. Some participants reported posting personal projects such as drawings and visual presentations, and reported that it made them feel good about themselves when people clicked "Like" in response to their posts.

Participants talked about the concept of being themselves online as opposed to portraying fake personas. They all explained that some of the people they knew were not always the same online as they were face-to-face, but that they (the participants) strove to be themselves when using media.

Entertainment and Distraction

All of the participants described media as being entertaining. Entertainment was one of the primary uses of media for most of the participants. They reported using media as a pastime and a diversion from boredom or negative feelings, and talked about the ways in which distraction could be positive. For example, Gloria said, "If you're depressed and you don't want to be depressed, you watch other people's lives and you don't think about yours at that time." She also talked about using media to pass the time while engaging in healthy activities. She stated:

> When you're watching TV and you're on any exercise machinery, the TV distracts you and sometimes you don't even realize that you're on it, because you're so into the TV. I recommend a lot of people try that instead of just sitting there.

While Gloria's statement about using media as a distraction when engaging in fitness activities coheres with the theme of "using media for good," it is used separately here to help demonstrate ways in which distractions can be positive.

Contrary to the concept of using media as a positive distraction, all of the participants expressed the role of media as a distraction from school work and other responsibilities. Sarah talked about media serving as a negative distraction as it pertained to academics and safety. She reported responding to her phone no matter what activity she was engaged in, and stated that there was nothing that could prevent her from picking up her phone whenever she heard message alerts. She explained that she could be doing her homework or even driving, and would stop and check her phone if she received a call or message alert. Sarah stated that when she was driving she often stopped or checked her phone while at a red light. She acknowledged the fact that she allowed media to distract her in negative ways. With the exception of texting and driving, many of the other participants discussed media as a negative distraction in a similar manner. Faith was the only participant who discussed making conscious efforts to limit distractions while studying and completing other important tasks. Faith stated that she often silenced her phone so she could focus on studying. She stated that even if she didn't turn her phone off, she focused on her academic work and allowed notifications to wait and not distract her. She also discussed using a "Do Not Disturb" feature that could be used to divert all phone alerts so she wouldn't feel obligated to respond to incoming calls and text messages.

Above the Influence

When asked about the influence of media on adolescent attitudes and behaviors, participants discussed media portrayals of negative behaviors and the tendency for teens their age to want to try many of those behaviors. They all stated that media influenced others, but most of them stated that they themselves did not follow or imitate bad behaviors observed via media. Most of the participants discussed the negative influence of media in the third person, as it did not pertain to them. For example, Felicity stated:

> They see others doing this or doing that and they think they're supposed to do that as well. They think that it's cool because they see other people posting pictures or videos of them doing negative things. They think that they're supposed to do that too, and sometimes media can make it come off as something positive, and really it's something negative.

Similarly, Sarah said:

> I think when they see a person and they're like smoking or something, a person tries, like peer pressure and stuff. Like if you see a person on the Internet and you see them doing something, you're like "I want to try that, too." I think that's how it can influence people. But as for me, no. I don't think Thus, because I know what I'm made of and I know what I can and can't do, so I wouldn't go follow somebody else.

Many of the other participants provided similar responses. Samantha talked about the possible influence of observing negative behaviors portrayed via media, but stated that she used media to influence her in positive ways. Samantha stated that media influenced her in good ways by teaching her right from wrong. When asked whether she thought media influenced teens her age to engage in negative behaviors, she said she believed it did.

When asked whether media influenced her in negative ways, she replied, "I see a lot of positivity on the Internet and I look at that a lot to influence myself if I'm ever down." Overall, the participants discussed the positive and negative influence of media along with their efforts to resist negative influences and practice positive behaviors.

Media Literacy on the Rise

Media literacy is education about the use and effects of media. This theme highlights the fact that efforts to promote media literacy have been useful. Each participant reported receiving advice about using media. They discussed ways in which media literacy was being promoted by parents, teachers, other adults in their lives, and even their peers. Most of the participants discussed the importance of protecting private information and not posting information that could compromise their identity or safety. They discussed the concept of digital footprints and the notion that things posted via social media would always exist and could be damaging to their chances of getting into college or getting jobs in the future. Participants reported that they had also received advice about limiting their use and practicing digital citizenship (e.g., kind behaviors) online.

Many of the students had taken some sort of computer-based classes and stated that their teachers discussed the importance of protecting information such as their social security numbers and their bank account information. All of the participants expressed concerns about violations of privacy and the presence of scams and hackers. One participant even talked about the presence of sex offenders and the risk of providing too much information online.

Gaining Awareness Through Monitoring and Reflection

The benefits of engaging in reflective activities such as journaling and interviews are well known (RobbGrieco & Hobbs, 2012; Stevens & Cooper, 2009). Correspondingly, each of the participants stated that participating in the research activities made them more aware of how much media they were consuming and how they spent their time. When asked what, if anything, they had learned from participating in the study, all of the participants said they realized they could benefit from decreasing their use of social media and increasing activities that pertained to their academic performance or future career. Participants also discussed the need to increase activities such as reading, playing instruments, building relationships, and volunteering for community service. Many of the participants said that completing and reviewing the media tracking activities helped them to realize how often they used social media and how they could benefit from using less media.

In addition to talking about what she had learned as a result of participating in the study, Sarah discussed realizations that occurred to her when she was not using her phone. She stated she believed she could exhibit better social and academic functioning if she didn't have her cell phone with her at all times. Jasmine discussed her realization that she engaged in the same media activities every day, and even when she was physically with other people she was not actually connecting with them due to her media use. She ended by saying, "This was an eye-opening experience." The participants' reports suggest that engaging teens in media monitoring activities was beneficial. Thus, it may be beneficial for counselors and other adults to share similar activities and discussions with teens who are heavily immersed in media.

Conclusion

Overall, participants discussed their views of the pros and cons of using media and reported that participating in the study made them more aware of their media use patterns and the effects of their media habits. Teens included in the current study and previous studies acknowledged the risks and negative occurrences involving media, but seemed to highlight positive factors. As indicated by the theme of "media literacy on the rise," each participant reported being informed about possible consequences of using and/or misusing media. All of the participants discussed media-related problems and negative occurrences they had either experienced or observed. Nonetheless, they remained optimistic about their use of media.

Despite the risks and negative experiences, participants enjoyed using media and maintained positive appraisals of media. They tended to emphasize the positive aspects. All of the participants emphasized ways in which they used media for positive purposes. Focusing on positive uses and having a positive outlook about media may help teens and adults to increase the benefits and gratifications associated with media. Likewise, promoting optimistic and positive uses of media may play a key role in reducing unhealthy media use and corresponding risks.

Of the risks and negative themes discussed by the participants, most related to concepts of time. It seems that while the practice of multitasking has increased, time and attention management has decreased. Throughout the interviews, participants discussed media as it related to concepts of distraction, procrastination, and interference. At the end of each interview, participants reported that they had realized how much time they displaced while using social media. They then discussed plans to make better use of their time.

At the end of the study, the researcher asked participants whether they had learned anything from participating in the study, and whether anything had occurred to them during the interview. Each participant reported that the study had helped them to realize how much media they were using and how they could use media in more productive ways. Most of the participants stated that, as a result of their participation, they planned to use less social media and increase academic, career, and extracurricular activities. A few participants stated that they would probably use just as much, or more, media in the near future, but each of them reported that they wanted to use media differently. One participant stated that the study was an "eye-opening experience." The other participants conveyed similar views of their participation in the study.

While the study offered valuable information, the research included limitations. One limitation of the study was the sample size of eight. The results of the study cannot be generalized to a larger population, but offer insight and understanding about adolescents' experiences and perspectives. Another limitation may stem from the fact that the study only included students who were willing to complete high-response activities. While previous literature has demonstrated a negative correlation between heavy media use and academic performance, most of the heavy media users included in the current study reported good grades. It is possible that students who were willing to track all of their media use for two days, keep a detailed journal for 14 days, and complete an hour-long interview were those who were high-achieving students. Many of the students who received recruitment packets were not selected to complete the interview because they failed to complete the high-response tracking and journal sheets. While many of them may have been heavy media users, the writing requirements may have deterred them from completing the study, and thus limited additional accounts that could have added to the findings. For future studies of this nature, it may be helpful to provide tracking and journal sheets with prefilled options as opposed to blank sheets that require time-consuming written responses.

Another limitation includes the study's reliance on self-report. The questions included in the interview asked participants to discuss the types of media they used, why they used and liked various types of media platforms, and how they thought media affected them in various areas. Dill (2009) discussed the idea that sometimes people don't really know why they do what they do, but are able to construct rational reasons to justify their decisions. Dill (2009) referenced an article by Nisbett and Wilson (1977) titled, "Telling More Than We Can Know: Verbal Reports on Mental Processes." The article demonstrated situations in which individuals were unable to accurately explain their behavior patterns when asked about the motives for their behaviors. For example, when asked to choose a favorite product, participants tended to choose the product furthest to the right, even when choices were identical. When participants were asked why a particular product was their favorite, they constructed explanations based on plausible causes as opposed to true introspection (Nisbett & Wilson, 1977). Nisbett and Wilson (1977) suggested that people may not have access to higher level mental processes, and may not be able to accurately report cognitive processes underlying their choices and behaviors. Thus, the reasoning participants provided about their media-related behaviors may not be accurate, and could be one of multiple plausible causes.

Furthermore, Dill (2009) discussed the tendency for people to believe that media did not affect them. She referenced the "third person affect," which was described as a phenomenon in which people believed other people were affected by media exposure, but they did not believe that they were personally affected. This coheres with the "Above the Influence" theme discussed in the previous chapter. Most of the participants agreed that media influenced teens their age, but stated they did not allow media to influence them in negative ways. It is possible that some participants may not know or want to admit to facts about their media-related choices and behaviors. To strengthen or explore the accuracy of self-reports in future research, self-reports about the use and influence of media may be supplemented with and compared to researcher observations of participants' social media content and reports from other people (e.g., participants' relatives, friends, and teachers). While participants' reports about the influence of media may be less than accurate, their responses represent their perspective of their experiences, and can be useful in providing insight into teens' experiences of their media world.

The aim of the current study was to describe participants' media habits and to qualitatively explore adolescents' perspectives about their experiences with media. It also aimed to facilitate activities and discussions that could help adolescents to increase awareness and critical thinking about their use of media, and help adults gain insight about areas in which teens may need guidance. The tracking and journaling activities were helpful in facilitating useful reflection among the teens, and the interview facilitated purposeful discussion between the researcher, a youth counselor, and the teens.   In addition to a deeper understanding of perspectives about positive uses of media, participants in the current study provided insight about the types of media-related guidance that might be useful to adolescents. The results of the current study suggest that positive media use can be used to promote education, health, and other aspects of well-being. The activities and the results of this study can be used by counselors, teachers, parents, pediatricians, and other adults who work with adolescents to promote academic development and psychosocial well-being.

Future Directions

Professionals and practitioners have used creative and expressive activities in conjunction with counseling and health services (Farrand, Perry, & Linsley, 2010). Writing in particular has been used in various forms of psychotherapy (Farrand, Perry, & Linsley, 2010). Art and expressive activities such as writing have been shown to support insight, coping, and personal growth (Lewis et al., 2005; Boniel-Nissim & Barak, 2011). The teens in the current study reported using music to improve their mood, videos to inspire and motivate themselves, and social media to seek social support. It is likely that healthy media use paired with expressive activities may provide many of the same benefits as art therapy. As social media evolves, future research on the effects of media should examine the therapeutic value of the use of specific media platforms among adolescents struggling with particular issues and health conditions.

Blogging is a form of digital journaling that allows users to express themselves, reflect on their thoughts, and share their writings with others. In addition to written text, bloggers may attach images, audio, video, or Web links to their posts. These additions, along with the interactive nature of blogs, may enhance the journaling experience and the therapeutic value of journaling for some. Blogging has been found to be helpful to people coping with various illnesses (Heilferty, 2009), trauma (Hoyt & Pasupathi, 2008), and social and emotional difficulties (Baker & Moore, 2011; Boniel-Nissim & Barak, 2013). Similarly, Tan (2008) and Hoyt and Pasupathi (2008) reported surveys that indicated many bloggers used blogs as a form of self-therapy. Knowledge gained about the effects of using specific platforms such as those related to blogging, music, videos, and social media may be applied to professional and health services. It might prove beneficial to examine the therapeutic value of specific types of media use among teens dealing with personal issues and health conditions.

References

American Academy of Pediatrics (n.d.). Retrieved from http://www.aap. org/en-us/Pages/Default.aspx

Baker, J. R., & Moore, S. M. (2011). An opportunistic validation of studies on the psychosocial benefits of blogging. *CyberPsychology, Behavior, and Social Networking, 14,* 387-390.

Boniel-Nissim, M., & Barak, A. (2013). The therapeutic value of adolescents' blogging about social-emotional difficulties. *Psychological Services, 10,* 333-341.

Dill, K. E. (2009). *How fantasy becomes reality: Seeing through media influence.* New York, NY: Oxford University Press.

Dominick, J. (1996). *The dynamics of mass communication* (5th ed.). New York, NY: McGraw-Hill.

Farrand, P., Perry, J. & Linsley, S. (2010). Enhancing self-practice/self-reflection (SP/SR) approach to cognitive behavioral training through the use of reflective blogs. *Behavioral and Cognitive Psychotherapy, 38,* 437-477.

Generations 2010. (2010). Retrieved from http://www.pewinternet. org/files/old-media/Files/Reports/2010/PIP_Generations_and_Tech10.pdf.

Heilferty, C. M. (2009). Toward a theory of online communication in illness: Concept analysis of illness blogs. *Journal of Advanced Nursing, 65,* 1539-1547.

Hoyt, T., & Pasupathi, M. (2008). Blogging about trauma: Linguistic markers of apparent recovery. *E-Journal of Applied Psychology, 4,* 56-62.

Lewis, R. J., Derlega, V. J., Clarke, E. G., Kuang, J. C., Jacobs, A.M, & McElligott, M. D. (2005). An expressive writing intervention to cope with lesbian-related stress: The moderating effects of openness about sexual orientation. *Psychology of Women Quarterly, 29,* 149-157.

Nisbett, R. E., & Wilson, T. D. (1977). Telling more than we can know: Verbal reports on mental processes. *Psychological Review, 84*(3),

231-259.

Rideout, V. J., Foehr, U. G., & Roberts, D. F. (2010). Generation M2: Media in the lives of 8-18 year olds. Retrieved from http://www.kff.org/entmedia/upload/8010.pdf.

Roberts, D. F., Henriksen, L., & Foehr, U. G. (2004). Adolescents and media. In R. M. Lerner & L. Steinberg (Eds.), *Handbook of adolescent psychology* (2nd ed., pp. 487-521). Hoboken, NJ: John Wiley & Sons.

RobbGrieco, M., & Hobbs, R. (2012). African-American children's active reasoning about media texts as a precursor to media literacy. *Journal of Children and Media, 6*(4), 502-519.

Stevens, D. D., & Cooper J. E. (2009). *Journal keeping: How to use reflective writing for learning, teaching, profession insight, and positive change*. Sterling, VA: Stylus.

Tan, L. (2008). Psychotherapy 2.0: Myspace blogging as self-therapy. *American Journal of Psychotherapy, 62*, 142-163.

About the Author

Dr. Yashica Holmes-Smith has worked as a counselor in academic, mental health, vocational, and hospital settings. In addition, she has taught psychology courses at colleges and universities. Yashica earned a B.A. in psychology from Georgia State University, an M.S. in applied clinical psychology from the University of South Carolina Aiken, and an M.A. and PhD in psychology with an emphasis in media psychology from Fielding Graduate University. Her passion for media arts and working with adolescents led her to found a nonprofit arts-based mentoring program for teen girls. Within the program, she uses media to connect with teens and to facilitate activities that supported teens' development of life skills and personal well-being. In addition, Yashica offers academic, career, and personal coaching services to adults. Her mission is to provide information and services that help individuals to develop skills and access resources that are supportive to their success and quality of life.

WHY EMOTIONAL PUBLIC SERVICE ANNOUNCEMENTS AFFECT THE BRAINS OF ADOLESCENTS DIFFERENTLY THAN THE BRAINS OF YOUNG ADULTS

Christophe Morin, PhD, Fielding Graduate University, USA

Abstract: Millions of dollars are spent each year to influence the behavioral health of adolescents and young adults via emotional public service announcements (PSAs). While the quantity of public health messages targeting these groups has increased, scholars and researchers are continuously questioning their effectiveness. Surprisingly, limited research has been conducted on the neurophysiological effect of PSAs and especially how brain-based persuasion models can explain the success or demise of many advertisements. Findings from this research show that adolescents use distinct brain circuits when processing emotional PSAs compared to young adults. It also suggests that persuasive messages do not work the same on the brains of adolescents compared to young adults. Specifically, the findings reveal that three conditions may impact the ultimate success of a PSA campaign on adolescents. The findings further reveal that neurodevelopmental differences between adolescents and young adults' brains may explain why PSAs with different formats and tones produce different neurophysiological responses between both groups. Undoubtedly, this research should help numerous organizations design better PSA campaigns to successfully warn and educate adolescents on many critical public health issues. Finally, the brain-based persuasion model proposed in this paper should provide better scientific evidence that strong visual warnings do work on adolescents, a fact that has been difficult to establish and sadly allowed tobacco companies to continuously block legislation mandating picture warnings on cigarette packaging.

Keywords: subliminal, advertising, adolescent, perception, public health, persuasion, PSA, neuromarketing, consumer neuroscience, media effect, media psychology, media neuroscience, brain-as-predictor

Introduction

Given the many lives that are at stake, reaching and persuading adolescents and young adults with regard to safety, education, and health issues, is a critical endeavor for our society. Yet while enormous amounts of funding are invested each year, public health advocates are actively demanding better persuasion models because most PSAs have little effect, or worse, even adverse effects in some cases. Emotions are critical mediators of how people process PSAs and, as such, play a central role in making any public health campaign compelling (Bagozzi, Gopinath, & Nyer, 1999). In fact, research has clearly demonstrated that effective advertising campaigns trigger strong emotional responses (Morris, Woo, Geason, & Kim, 2002).

So how do emotional appeals affect the persuasive strength of a PSA? What is the biological logic followed by the brain during an emotional event? Are there key age differences in brain circuitry that affect the way adolescents respond to an emotional message compared to young adults? Until the early 1990s, most persuasion models consistently underplayed the influence of subconscious emotional factors (Johar, Maheswaran, & Peracchio, 2006). But recent studies conducted by consumer neuroscientists have confirmed that subconscious affective processes are key drivers of emotional responses and behaviors. While the evidence that has emerged is now overwhelming, few public health scholars and researchers have fully embraced this new body of knowledge. Some clearly struggle with the difficulty of integrating neuroscientific protocols into PSA studies, while others consider the use of medical technologies to study media effects too controversial (Murphy, Illes, & Reiner, 2008).

How do emotional appeals affect the persuasive strength of a PSA?

While the volume of papers discussing the persuasive effectiveness of public health campaigns on youth is impressive, a review of the top categories of PSAs (anti-tobacco, obesity, and drugs) reveals that creative development is rarely guided by the use of persuasion models. In fact, less than one-third of empirical articles about PSA campaigns report using any theory at all (Randolph & Viswanath, 2004). Moreover, the models most commonly used are based on old cognitive theoretical frameworks that tend to exaggerate the importance of conscious processes mediating how persuasion works (Brehm & Brehm, 1981; Dickinson & Holmes, 2008; Donohew, Lorch, & Palmgreen, 1998; Hastings, Stead, & Webb, 2004; Lang, 2000; Maddux & Rogers, 1983; Palmgreen, Donohew, Lorch, Hoyle, & Stephenson, 2001; Petty, Cacioppo, & Heesacker, 1981; Rosenblatt, Greenberg, Solomon, Pyszczynski, & Lyon, 1989; Rothman, Martino, Bedell, Detweiler, & Salovey, 1999; Witte & Allen, 2000).

Furthermore, studies on PSA effectiveness report outcomes that differ sharply from each other, making it difficult for researchers to understand why some campaigns work while a majority of others don't (Fishbein, Hall-Jamieson, Zimmer, von Haeften, & Nabi, 2002). In addition, many health advocates continue to use theoretical frameworks borrowed from the field of behavioral health, confirming that the most important objective of a campaign is often to address the dysfunctional behavior rather than focus on the persuasive effectiveness of the PSA. A meta-review of 15 persuasion models most frequently used in public health campaigns reveals a high level of confusion and discord among media researchers and public health advocates alike (Noar, 2006). Meanwhile, PSA campaigns that do show success are more likely to apply a specific persuasion model and to rely on triggering a strong emotional response.

What is the biological logic followed by the brain during an emotional event?

Multiple studies conducted in personality neuroscience, cognitive neuroscience, affective neuroscience, neuroeconomics, and neuromarketing have solidly confirmed the existence of a dynamic relationship between changes in emotional states and changes in neurophysiology (DeYoung et al., 2010; Gazzaniga, Ivry, & Mangun, 2009; Glimcher, 2009; Langleben et al., 2009; Tamietto & de Gelder, 2010).

Fundamentally, the biological reason why emotions have such a profound effect on behavior is that they quickly change our state of homeostasis, a state of physiological equilibrium people seek naturally to maintain. Emotions can raise the heart rate (HR), increase blood pressure, and disrupt other autonomic functions such as sleep, perspiration, respiration, and even digestion. Multiple brain structures are involved in this process, but the limbic system (subcortical) is considered largely responsible for managing emotions. Interestingly, there are more fibers projecting from the limbic area to the frontal lobe than the other way around, suggesting the critical importance and dominance of subconscious mechanisms in emotional processing functions. In fact, Panksepp, a prominent affective neuroscientist, claims that our emotional responses are purely instinctual rather than learned (Panksepp, 2004).

Are there key age differences in emotional systems between adolescents and young adults?

Increasingly, research suggests that persuasive messages have the power to activate reward circuits that may be more sensitive in adolescents' brains than they are in adult brains. Hence, a growing number of advertising researchers are supporting the notion that adolescents are more vulnerable to the effect of advertising in general because of the distinct sensitivity of their subcortical structures (Pechmann, Levine, Loughlin, & Leslie, 2005). Specifically, several studies have shown distinct patterns of brain activity between adolescents and adults when anticipating gains or losses. Indeed, it appears that adolescents have biological predispositions to activating brain areas involved in short-term rewards and risk avoidance when placed in emotional situations (Cauffman et al., 2010; Ernst et al., 2005; Figner, Mackinlay, Wilkening, & Weber, 2009; Galvan, Hare, Voss, Glover, & Casey, 2007; Lau et al., 2011). Basically, adolescents have heightened sensitivity to reward, reduced sensitivity to punishment, and an inferior capacity to exercise cognitive control over impulsivity.

While emotions undoubtedly play a strong role in PSAs' effectiveness, researchers have long struggled to measure the strength and direction of an emotional response. Conventional methods rely heavily on self-reports and observations, and therefore often fail to provide reliable measures of the biological mechanism underlying an emotional response. However, ad studies conducted by consumer neuroscientists, neuromarketers, and neuroeconomists have demonstrated that it is possible to generate valuable insights from biometric and neurologic data (DeYoung et al., 2010; Glimcher, 2009; Tamietto & de Gelder, 2010).

Conceptual Framework

Because emotional messages do differently affect adolescents and adults in ways that are not clearly understood, the purpose of this paper is to present scientific insights addressing a critical research question:

Are there neurophysiological differences between late adolescents and young adults when viewing public service announcements (PSAs) that vary in emotional tone and appeal to different consciousness levels?

First, because brain maturation is considered complete at around 24 years of age, the sample for this study was composed of two groups of 36 subjects: A group of late adolescents who were either 18, 19, or 20 years of age and a group of young adults between the ages of 25 and 45. Second, the PSAs featured three major public health issues (Morin, 2012): drug abuse; drinking and driving; and texting and driving. The PSAs addressed each of the three issues in two different tones: (a) a positive tone using humor; and (b) a negative tone using fear and blame. Finally, the taxonomy proposed by Dehaene et al. provided an effective way to categorize the emotional messages used in the study in terms of how they would activate distinct brain states (Dehaene, Changeux, Naccache, Sackur, & Sergent, 2006). As a result, three formats of messages were prepared: (a) a conscious format (CF); (b) a preconscious format (PF); and (c) a subliminal format (SF).

In their breakthrough model, Dehaene et al. proposed that the state of vigilance can explain the different states of consciousness. Vigilance is defined as a continuous variable that encompasses wakefulness, sleep, coma, and anesthesia. According to the researchers, as vigilance rises, the brain recruits more brain areas requiring cerebral blood flow, a phenomena that can be tracked easily through an *f*MRI. Meanwhile, the top-down attention effect of consciousness is what gives rise to information awareness, a process that typically propagates throughout the brain (Figure 1). On the other hand, the bottom-up effect characterizes a situation in which unconscious brain activity is triggered through strong emotional events.

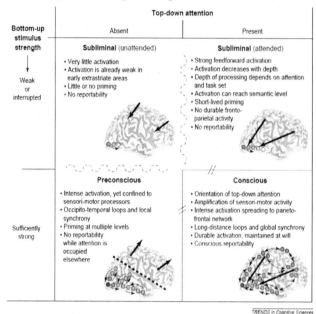

Figure 1. Dehaene et al.'s model of consciousness

A CF PSA was presented as a 30-second video on a computer screen (see Figure 2):

Figure 2. A fear-provoking conscious format PSA

A PF preconscious format PSA was slightly smaller than the CF format and the video player was embedded in an image representing a YouTube browser. Additionally, a banner ad relevant to the public health theme was displayed for only five seconds in the lower right corner of the screen when the video was played (see Figure 3). The banner ad presented a second visual stimulus, thus creating a context in which information could only be attended to with partial or covert attention. A negative PSA was paired with a negative banner ad (Figure 3), while a positive PSA was paired with a positive banner ad (Figure 4). Before viewing a PF PSA, subjects were specifically instructed to concentrate on the main clip, but it was expected that the banner ad displayed for five seconds would nonetheless be processed by their covert attention system.

Figure 3. A preconscious PSA with a negative banner ad

Figure 4. A preconscious PSA with a positive banner ad

An SF PSA was created as a 30-second video clip in which a positive or negative visual frame was flashed for approximately 40 milliseconds (Figure 5 and Figure 6), a speed considered to be the threshold of visual consciousness—that is, subliminal. A negative subliminal prime was paired with a negative PSA, while a positive subliminal prime was paired with a positive PSA. A two-minute clip featuring a white cross was viewed by each participant before each PSA to reset neurophysiological biomarkers (Figure 7).

Figure 5. Fear-provoking

Figure 6. Hopeful

Figure 7. Cross point video frame

The neurophysiological effect of positive and negative PSAs was assessed by using a mix of research methods measuring the degree to which all six PSAs would produce arousal (emotional intensity), at what valence (positive vs. negative), and to which extent the message was encoded and would influence people to donate.

Research Methods and Constructs

There are several methods that can record emotional changes (arousal and valence) produced by conscious, subliminal, or preconscious messages. The study relied on methods monitoring the autonomic response system (ANS) to explain the neurophysiological effect of the emotional PSAs.

What is the autonomic nervous system (ANS)?

Three anatomical subdivisions control and monitor the way people respond to any stimuli: the central nervous system (CNS); the peripheral nervous system (PNS); and the autonomic nervous system (ANS). The ANS works on autopilot to regulate critical survival functions (e.g., respiration, digestion, heart rate, temperature, sweating, etc.). ANS activity can signal critical affective, cognitive, and behavioral shifts (Mendes, 2009). Because the speed at which the ANS reacts is well below our awareness, activity of the ANS is a good candidate to measure responses to subliminal or preconscious messages (Bechara, Damasio, Tranel, & Damasio, 1997; Ravaja, 2004). Three of the best methods to observe changes in the ANS are electrodermal activity (EDA), heart rate variability (HRV), and respiratory sinus arrhythmia (RSA).

EDA is designed to measure the response of eccrine glands, which are the sweats glands found in virtually all of our skin and are most numerous in the palms of our hands and the soles of our feet. These glands are very sensitive to external and internal stimuli. EDA is calculated by measuring the variation of a constant electrical current passing through the skin. HRV activity or the measure of vagal tone (also known as parasympathetic tone) directly correlates to how the peripheral nervous system (PNS) responds to inhibit high states of arousal; therefore, it is an important measure of how much a subject can maintain or restore a state of homeostasis during an experiment. RSA measures the changes in the R-spike that are produced during breathing and is a common way to measure parasympathetic tone. The RSA cycle provides critical information on the degree to which the parasympathetic and sympathetic branches of the nervous system are active during the processing of emotional stimuli.

Measuring arousal

Arousal is intimately related to the entire activity of our sensory system. The measurement of excitatory or inhibitory reactions in our physiology has been possible for decades and is typically measured by conducting electrophysiological research (DeYoung & Gray, 2009). The region of the brain that is considered responsible for how individuals orient their attention is a subcortical area called the thalamus, and it can signal low or high arousal states. In the thalamus, special neurons called attention-grabbing neurons (AGN) are highly sensitive to visual stimulation (Lesica & Stanley, 2004). Visual response is a key component of how emotions affect the brain. In fact, approximately 55% of the cortical surface—more than any other sense—is dedicated to vision-related processing (Kolb & Whishaw, 2009). In addition, since an estimated 10% of our optic nerves connecting the eyes to the brain end in a subcortical structure called the superior colliculus (SC, see Figure 1), the mechanism by which people orient their visual attention is largely subconscious.

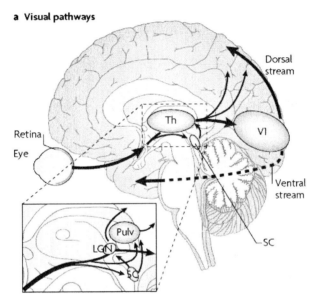

Figure 8. Unconscious visual pathway (Dehaene & Changeux, 2005)

Assessing valence

Valence represents the direction of an emotional state and is mediated by many neurochemicals such as neurotransmitters, neuropeptides, and hormones. These chemicals activate brain circuitry when people experience fear, surprise, or laughter to quickly orient the reaction toward or away from a stimulus. Humans have a range of approximately 18,000 emotions (Plutchik, 1991), but we typically activate a limited set of these emotions, sometimes referred to as primal emotions, on a daily basis (Panksepp, 1998). These emotions have distinct patterns of neurophysiological responses and are known to produce universal facial expressions (Ekman &

Friesen, 1971; Hess, 2009).

Encoding information in the brain

Though it is still very difficult to crack the neural code of encoding in general, it is clear that subcortical areas of the brain such as the hippocampus have an important role in creating and maintaining our long-term memories (Carlson, 2007). Also, research conducted by Bogdan Draganski and his colleagues (2006) demonstrated that gray matter volume increases as a result of learning, offering scientists more tangible ways to measure the neuroanatomical correlates of memory. Meanwhile, several neuromarketing studies have also shown that the frontal lobes play a large role in strengthening or weakening retention of an advertising message, and that memory of an ad correlates positively with the probability of selecting a brand (Rossiter, Silberstein, Harris, & Nield, 2001; Tusche, Bode, & Haynes, 2010).

Behavioral measurement

In this study, the behavioral effect of the PSAs was measured by the amount of the donations participants made to support each public health issue. The decision to make a voluntary donation activates brain regions similar to other basic valuations involving rewards (Hare, Camerer, Knoepfle, D'Doherty, & Rangel, 2010); therefore it is a good measure of the persuasive effect of a PSA.

Research Hypotheses

The key research hypotheses were as follows:

- H1: PSAs with humorous tones produce different neurophysiological and behavioral effects on late adolescents (YG) compared to young adults (AG).
- H2: PSAs with fear-provoking tones produce different neurophysiological and behavioral effects on late adolescents compared to young adults.
- H3: PSAs presented in the conscious format (CF) produce different neurophysiological and behavioral effects on late adolescents compared to young adults.

- H4: PSAs presented in the preconscious format (PF) produce different neurophysiological and behavioral effects on late adolescents compared to young adults.
- H5: PSAs presented in the subliminal format (SF) produce different neurophysiological and behavioral effects on late adolescents compared to young adults.

Findings

Based on the data of this experiment, the null hypothesis for H1 was accepted because the difference between the adolescent group and the young adult group was not significant across the three positive messages. The null hypothesis for H2 was also accepted because the difference between the adolescent group and the young adult group was not significant across all three negative messages tested. However, the negative messages consistently produced higher effect scores than the positive messages did as measured by both self-reported and biometric data. This does suggest that negative messages produce larger emotional effects than positive messages overall, regardless of the age of the subjects. The null hypothesis for H3 was rejected because CF messages did produce statistically different neurophysiological and behavioral effects on young adults than on late adolescents. The CF PSAs produced slightly more effect one the young adult group than on the adolescent group. However, the level of contrast between both groups was consistently less than the level of contrast identified for the other two formats. The null hypothesis was also rejected for H4. PSAs in the preconscious format did produce significantly more neurophysiological effect on young adults than on late adolescents. However, the level of contrast created by PF messages on both groups was consistently lower than the level of contrast identified for either CF or SF. Finally, the null hypothesis was rejected for H5 because SF messages did produce significantly higher neurophysiological and behavioral effects on adolescents than on young adults. More importantly, the level of contrast created by SF was consistently higher than for the other two formats.

The following two tables present the study's dependent variables and what they measured. Surveys were conducted before and after viewing the PSAs to obtain self-reported emotional responses to the PSAs as well as to assess retention levels (encoding). All self-reported variables are listed in Table 1, while biometric variables are presented in Table 2. The statistical power of all of the tests performed during this study was greater than 80% unless otherwise specified. This level represents a standard threshold to avoid making type II errors (false negatives).

Table 1
Self-reported Variable

Variable Name	Measuring	Proxy for
SR-emo	Emotional intensity after each PSA	Emotional arousal
SR-impact	Intentional impact after each PSA	Emotional arousal
Ratings 1	Ranking of each PSA after viewing all six	Valence
Ratings 2	Rankings of each PSA 2 weeks after viewing	Valence
Ratings Delta	Differences in ranking PSAs after viewing and after two weeks	Utility
Recall 1	Memorization right after viewing each PSA	Short-term encoding
Recall 2	Memorization of each PSA after two weeks	Long-term encoding
Donations	Contribution towards each cause featured in each PSA	Behavior

Table 2 provides a summary description of the 24 (8 types x 3 formats) biometric variables and their potential value for assessing specific neuro-physiological states.

Table 2
Biometric Variables

Variable name	Measuring	Proxy for
EDA	Skin conductance level (SLC) change right after the start of the PSA	Arousal
EDA 2	SLC average change two seconds after the start of the PSA	Arousal
NS_SCR	Number of nonspecific events	Valence
HR	Heart rate	Valence
R-R	Heart beats interval data	Arousal
RR	Breadth per minute	Valence
RSA	Changes in respiration spikes	Valence
Vagal	Vagal tone	Emotional control

The following charts offer a visual representation of the main effects measured during the experiment. Figure 9 shows the effect sizes for all self-reported variables on the different categories of interest (format, tone, age, and their interaction). An effect below 0.2 is considered small; between .2 and .4, the effect is considered medium; and above 4 the effect is considered large.

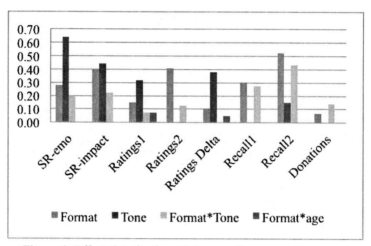

Figure 9. Effect data for format, tone, and age on self-reported dependent variable

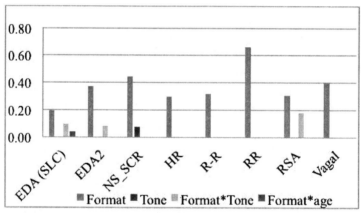

Figure 10. Effect data for format, tone, and age on biometric dependent variable

Figure 10 shows the effect sizes of all biometric variables for the different categories of interest (format, tone, age, and their interaction). This chart shows that format did produce medium to large effects on all biometric variables. Figure 11 shows the effect of each format on key dependent variables. This chart shows that the SF format generated far more effect than any other format.

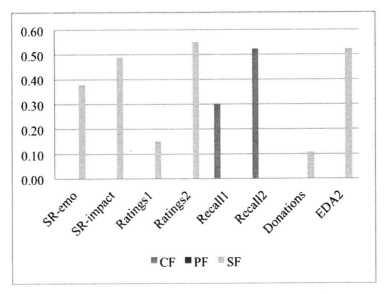

Figure 11. Effect of format on key dependent variables

Figure 12 shows the effects between the interaction of the SF format and the negative tone, the CF format and the positive tone, and the SF format and age. The chart shows a medium effect for recall of the CF format in a positive tone.

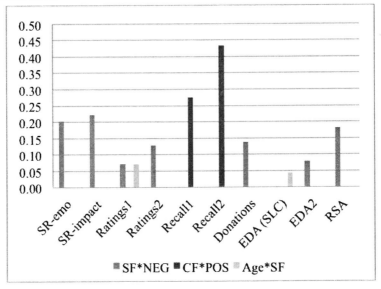

Figure 12. Effect of the interaction between tone, format, and age

Conclusions

In the last decade, changes in the media landscape have put excessive pressure on media scholars to improve persuasion theories. For too long, popular persuasion models such as the elaboration likelihood model (ELM)
have failed to integrate bio-psychological mechanisms (Ravaja, 2004). In
fact, Petty and his colleagues have admitted that "there might still be some
potentially hidden, persuasive effects on the automatic evaluative associations . . . which are simply not captured by the model" (Petty, Brinol, &
Priester, 2009, p. 149). Surprisingly, no research paper has yet specifically
addressed the effect PSAs have on adolescent brains, a fact that has often
been cited as a critical flaw by researchers. Additionally, PSA research
involving adolescents has not convincingly explained its own findings.
For instance, it is unclear why health campaigns directed toward youth
appear to have little or less success compared to those directed toward
parents or adults (Derzon & Lipsey, 2002). Researchers such as Palmgreen
and his colleagues even claim that some campaigns targeting adolescents
fail because they produce a "mysterious effect" they call "the widespread
phenomenon effect" (Palmgreen et al., 2001). Under this cryptic phenomenon, adolescents may perceive frequent exposure to a campaign against
drugs or tobacco as evidence that the practice is more widespread than
they previously thought. They further speculate that adolescents engage in
such behavior in order to increase peer acceptance. Meanwhile, research
investigating the effect of anti-tobacco campaigns on a large sample of
adolescents has found that the level of reactance to a campaign appears
to increase with age. According to the researchers, this a fact is strongly
supported by the reactance theory (Grandpre, Alvaro, Burgoon, Miller, &
Hall, 2003). However, the researchers in the same study failed to provide a convincing theoretical framework explaining why implicit (i.e.,
mostly processed subconsciously) anti-tobacco messages were more effective than explicit messages, regardless of the tone of the message (for
or against tobacco). Likewise, studies have shown that ads focusing on
the negative short-term life circumstances of smoking have brought good
results, but the emotional and cognitive data are considered limited be-

cause it is only based on self-reported assessments made by adolescents (Sutfin, Szykman, & Moore, 2008). Finally, graphic warning labels work better than text-only labels to reduce the social appeal of cigarettes on adolescents, and campaigns that emphasize the health benefits of "eating right" or "exercising more" do not work (Austin, 1995). However, none of the persuasion models discussing these findings are supported by a solid understanding of the differential effect of these stimuli on the brains of the participants.

Thus, this study confirms the importance and value of conducting more media experiments measuring the neurophysiological effect of PSAs on the brain of adolescents. It further establishes that the neurodevelopmental differences between adolescents and young adults can explain why PSAs produce neurophysiological differences between both groups. Specifically, the findings reveal that three conditions may impact the ultimate success of a PSA campaign.

PSAs that are processed mostly consciously produce less effect on adolescents

This can be explained by the fact that adolescents have a less mature prefrontal cortex, which means that they naturally dedicate less focused attention than young adults and exert less affective control while viewing PSAs. This finding also suggests that PSAs targeting adolescents should use less data, less text, and even less voice over because these message elements require more cognitive effort than visual stimuli. Meanwhile, to trigger strong emotional responses from an adolescent brain requires more stimulation than doing so with young adults.

PSAs that are processed mostly preconsciously produce less effect on adolescents

The consciousness model proposed by Dehaene supports the theoretical perspective that a message appealing to a preconscious state may have a more potent effect on an adult brain than on a young brain because of maturation differences in the prefrontal cortex. For a preconscious message to "radiate" upward, it needs to recruit and amplify weak activation of the subcortical circuitry. If such circuitry is not fully mature, preconscious activity may not receive the critical boost from the most evolved part of the brain (the cortex), a brain layer that controls focus and concentration. This suggests that any form of PSA campaign built on targeting the covert attention of adolescents will not perform well. Banner ads and product placements typically fall into that category.

PSAs that are processed mostly subconsciously produce more effects on the adolescent brain

This difference may be explained by the relative dominance of the subcortical circuitry in the adolescent brain, one that is responsible for activating the bottom-up process (subcortical to cortical). This preference may also explain why subliminal primes produce more arousal on adolescents. Indeed, adolescent brains rely excessively on the subcortical circuitry to process emotional events and recruit limited cognitive resources (compared to adults) to mediate conscious responses. In the absence of a fully evolved prefrontal cortex, adolescents are faster at processing subliminal emotional messages, a response characterized by a surge in arousal (higher EDA) and higher donations. As noted in the literature review, during a subconscious state of awareness, the possibility for the receiver to control and regulate the response to an emotional appeal is considerably reduced (Carlson, 2007; Gazzaniga et al., 2009). With an understanding that using subliminal primes in PSA campaigns is not an acceptable approach, we can see that this finding points to the importance of media production techniques that are known to impact a viewer at the threshold of visual consciousness, such as using a rapid succession of frame changes, featuring strong facial expressions, and creating narrative arcs that produce fast and potent emotional lifts. This further implies that, to be effective, PSAs targeting adolescents need to create higher sensation value (HSV) than those targeting young adults, a fact that has been confirmed by *f*MRI research conducted on smokers viewing anti-tobacco ads (Wang et al., 2013).

Tone differences

While this experiment did not yield conclusive evidence regarding the relative difference between age groups with respect to message tone, it identified qualitative trends suggesting that negative messages do produce higher emotional states overall compared to positive messages. This may be explained because of biological priorities set at a primal level in the subcortical brain areas to ensure that threats are processed with greater urgency and importance than positive messages. Considering that many public health campaigns use negative appeals but others don't, this confirmation is a critical piece of qualitative evidence that suggests negative appeals produce more persuasive effect than positive appeals and could be used with more confidence as a dominant tone in future PSA campaigns.

Using a neurophysiological model of persuasion (NMP) to produce better public health campaigns

Developing effective public health campaigns has been a big challenge for health advocates for decades. Many scholars have tried to assess the effectiveness of these campaigns, but the lack of discipline and consistency in creating and deploying these efforts has made this endeavor extremely difficult (Evans, Blitstein, Hersey, Renaud, & Yaroch, 2008; Randolph & Viswanath, 2004). A common problem facing the producers of PSAs in general is to adopt a persuasion model that can produce accurate predictions. For instance, the literature review on the subject suggests that there are conflicting positions regarding the degree to which campaigns should use negative (fear-based) or positive (reward-based) appeals (Witte & Allen, 2000). As a result, many campaigns struggle to find a consistent and effective creative tone. This new piece of research provides critical insights that can help integrate self-reported data, biometric data, and behavioral data for the purpose of assessing and predicting the effectiveness of emotional PSAs on adolescents and young adults. This model belongs to a growing family of integrated persuasion models influenced by neuroscience. Such models are currently gaining growing attention as findings from neuromarketing and neuroecononomics studies continue to establish the relevance and value of brain-based methods (Breiter et al., 2015).

The five variables of this neurophysiological persuasion model (NMP) represent key aspects of how messages affect conscious, preconscious, and subconscious processes in the brain. Aa According to the NMP, the persuasive effect of a PSA campaign is a function of four critical dependent variables.

PE (Persuasive Effect) = f(A (arousal) X R (rating) X B (behavior) x M (memorization), whereas:

- A is measured by EDA (subconscious)
- R is measured by self-reported preference (conscious)
- B is measured by donation (conscious)
- M is measured by recall (subconscious, preconscious and conscious)

While the bulk of American public health campaigns continue to use older persuasion models anchored in rational-centric psychological theories, few have implemented campaigns that aim to systematically captivate and impress adolescents both consciously and subconsciously. By integrating neurophysiological and self-reported variables, NMP should encourage PSA producers to use more negative appeals. According to NMP, fear-based PSAs do create the strongest effects on both adolescents and young adults' brains and can be paired with strong calls to action to influence behavioral change.

In the United States, attempts to use negative ways to appeal to adolescents have been facing legal challenges from advertisers on all fronts. The most publicized case is the legal battle between the U.S. government and the tobacco industry. For decades, the tobacco industry has insisted that they should enjoy the freedom to communicate with their customers, and therefore they violently oppose negative associations. In 2011, the U.S. government adopted the use of "picture warnings" on packs of cigarettes (McKay & Kesmodel, 2011) because they have been recommended by the World Health Organization for years and are known to work much better than just text warnings to deter young smokers (WHO, 2012). Yet a U.S. court opposed the move, not only because these warnings violate corporate free speech rights but because the scientific evidence supporting the fact that these graphic warnings (Figure 13) are effective was considered "too weak" (Reuters, 2012). Fortunately, the research presented in this paper produces strong evidence supporting the use of such warnings to deter adolescents and should help the U.S. government in its endeavor to produce scientific evidence that can challenge the tobacco industry.

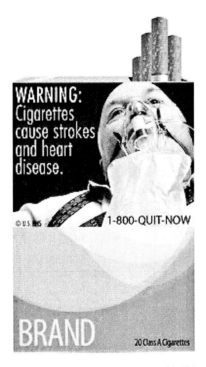

Figure 13. Graphic warning proposed by the FDA

In summary, this research provides a better understanding of the mechanism underlying how PSAs influence the brains of adolescents and young adults. Many public health scholars have long asked for additional research to be conducted in this area in order to improve the protection of adolescents (Berry & McMullen, 2008; Chester, Montgomery, & Dorfman, 2010; Friestad & Wright, 2005; Montgomery & Chester, 2008, 2011; Nairn, 2009; Nairn & Fine, 2008; Pechmann et al., 2005; Strasburger, 2009; Strasburger, Jordan, & Donnerstein, 2009; Walsh & Gentile, 2003). Undoubtedly, this research can help numerous organizations design better campaigns in order to warn and educate adolescents on the dangers of consuming alcohol, using tobacco, texting while driving, and eating junk food, as well as many other critical public health issues. Meanwhile, this research may also help accelerate the legal adoption of effective communication techniques warning young consumers of the health risks of products such as tobacco that have been legally blocked by advertisers for decades.

Recommendations for Future Research

Considering that the scope of the current study was to make valuable contributions to a field of study that is in its infancy, there are clear limitations to its external validity.

Increase Sample Size

Clearly, this is a relatively easy variable to control. The research was performed on a relatively small sample of 72 participants, which limits its ability to deliver statistics with high levels of confidence and statistical power. When using biometric data, effect sizes are typically small; therefore, using large samples would deliver better power.

Increase Message Themes

While it was rather challenging to find three themes that were each developed using both a negative and a positive tone, future research should investigate the possibility of using more themes created in both tones. The option of producing messages that are specifically scripted around negative or positive narratives for the purpose of testing them should be explored. Also, there would be value in testing the emotional effects using the NMP model for campaigns that mix tones and formats.

Add Neurophysiological Protocols

While the choice of focusing on a mix of methods known to measure the ANS was supported by the theoretical perspective, it would have been very valuable to add EEGs or eye tracking to this research. EEGs would provide another way to measure the effects of both format and tone, while eye-tracking data would deliver valuable insights on the critical visual elements that recruit the highest attention, especially in the presence of preconscious ads.

Extend the Timeframe of the Experiment

The period used in our experiment was only two weeks. Future research should consider using a longer timeframe, especially to measure the degree to which encoding lasts for each format and tone.

References

Austin, E. W. (1995). Reaching young audiences: Developmental considerations in designing health messages. In E. Maibach & R. Parrott (Eds.), *Designing health messages: Approaches from communication theory and public health practice* (pp. 114-144). Thousand Oaks, CA: Sage.

Bagozzi, R. P., Gopinath, M., & Nyer, P. U. (1999). The role of emotions in marketing. *Journal of the Academy of Marketing Science, 27*(2), 184-206.

Bechara, A., Damasio, H., Tranel, D., & Damasio, A. R. (1997). Deciding advantageously before knowing the advantageous strategy. *Science, 275*, 1293-1294.

Berridge, K. C. (2004). Motivation concepts in behavioral neuroscience. *Physiology & Behavior, 81*, 179-209.

Berry, B., & McMullen, T. (2008). Visual communication to children in the supermarket context: Health protective or exploitive. *Agriculture and Human Values, 25*, 333-348.

Brehm, S., & Brehm, J. (1981). *Psychological reactance: A theory of freedom and control.* New York: Academic Press.

Breiter, H. C., Block, M., Blood, A. J., Calder, B., Chamberlain, L., Lee, N., . . . Zhang, F. (2015). Redefining neuromarketing as an integrated science of influence. *Frontiers in Human Neuroscience, 8,* 1-7.

Bryant, J., & Oliver, M. B. (2009). *Media effects: Advances in theory and research* (3rd ed.). New York, NY: Routledge.

Carlson, N. R. (2007). *Physiology of behavior* (9th ed.). Boston, MA: Pearson Education.

Casey, B. J., Jones, R. M., & Hare, T. H. (2008). The adolescent brain. *Annals of the New York Academy of Sciences, 1124*(1), 111-126.

Cauffman, E., Shulman, E. P., Steinberg, L., Claus, E., Banich, M. T., Graham, S., & Woolard, J. (2010). Age differences in affective decision making as indexed by performance on the Iowa Gambling Task. *Developmental Psychology, 46*(1), 193-207. doi:10.1037/a0016128

Chester, J., Montgomery, K., & Dorfman, L. (2010). *Alcohol marketing in the digital age*. Retrieved from http://www.digitalads.org/documents/BMSG-CDD-Digital-Alcohol-Marketing.pdf.

Dehaene, S., Changeux, J., Naccache, L., Sackur, J., & Sergent, C. (2006). Conscious, preconscious, and subliminal processing: A testable taxonomy. *Trends in Cognitive Sciences, 10*(5), 204-211.

Derzon, J. H., & Lipsey, M. W. (2002). A meta-analysis of the effectiveness of mass-communication for changing substance-use knowledge, attitudes, and behavior. In W. D. Crano & M. Burgoon (Eds.), *Mass media and drug prevention: Classic and contemporary theories and research* (pp. 231-258). Mahwah, NJ: Lawrence Erlbaum Associates.

DeYoung, C. G., & Gray, J. R. (2009). Personality neuroscience: Explaining individual differences in affect, behavior, and cognitio. In P. J. Corr & G. Matthews (Eds.), *Cambridge handbook of personality psychology* (pp. 323-346). New York, NY: Cambridge University Press.

DeYoung, C. G., Hirsh, J. B., Shane, M. S., Papademetris, X., Rajeevan, N., & Gray, J. R. (2010). Testing predictions from personality neuroscience: Brain structure and the Big Five. *Psychological Science, 21*(6), 820-828.

Dickinson, S., & Holmes, M. (2008). Understanding the emotional and coping responses of adolescent individuals exposed to threat appeals. *International Journal of Advertising, 27*(2), 251-278.

Dobbs, D. (2011). Beautiful teenage brains. *National Geographic, 220*, 36-59.

Donohew, L., Lorch, E. P., & Palmgreen, P. (1998). Applications of a theoretic model of information exposure to health interventions. *Human Communication Research, 24*(3), 454-468.

doi:10.1111/j.1468-2958.1998.tb00425.x

Draganski, B., Gaser, C., Kempermann, G., Kuhn, H. G., Winkler, J., Buchel, C., & May, A. (2006). Temporal and spatial dynamics of brain structure changes during extensive learning. *The Journal of Neuroscience, 26*(23), 6314-6317.

Ekman, P., & Friesen, W. V. (1971). Constants across cultures in the face and emotion. *Journal of Personality and Social Psychology, 17*, 124-129. Retrieved from https://www.paulekman.com/wp-content/uploads/2013/07/Constants-Across-Cultures-In-The-Face-And-Emotion.pdf.

Ernst, M., Nelson, E. E., Jazbec, S., McClure, E. B., Monk, C. S., Leibenluft, E., . . . Pine, D. S. (2005). Amygdala and nucleus accumbens in responses to receipt and omission of gains in adults and adolescents. *Neuroimage, 25*(4), 1279-1291. doi:10.1016/j.neuroimage.2004.12.038

Evans, W. D., Blitstein, J., Hersey, J., Renaud, J., & Yaroch, A. (2008). Systematic review of public health branding. *Journal of Health Communication, 13*(8), 721-741. doi:10.1080/10810730802487364

Figner, B., Mackinlay, R. J., Wilkening, F., & Weber, E. U. (2009). Affective and deliberative processes in risky choice: Age differences in risk taking in the Columbia Card Task. *Journal of Experimental Psychology-Learning Memory and Cognition, 35*(3), 709-730. doi:10.1037/a0014983

Fishbein, M., Hall-Jamieson, K., Zimmer, E., von Haeften, I., & Nabi, R. (2002). Avoiding the boomerang: Testing the relative effectiveness of antidrug public service announcements before a national campaign. *American Journal of Public Health, 92*(2), 238-245. doi:10.2105/ajph.92.2.238

Friestad, M., & Wright, P. (2005). The next generation: Research for twenty-first century policy on children and advertising. *American Marketing Association, 24*(2), 183-185.

Galvan, A., Hare, T., Voss, H., Glover, G., & Casey, B. J. (2007). Risk-taking and the adolescent brain: Who is at risk? *Developmental*

Science, 10(2), F8-F14. doi:10.1111/j.1467-7687.2006.00579.x

Gazzaniga, M. S., Ivry, R. B., & Mangun, G. R. (2009). *Cognitive neuro-science: The biology of the mind* (Third Edition ed.). New York, NY: W.W. Norton.

Glimcher, P. W. (2009). *Neuroeconomics: Decision-making and the brain.* London, UK: Elsevier.

Grandpre, J., Alvaro, E. M., Burgoon, M., Miller, C. H., & Hall, J. R. (2003). Adolescent reactance and anti-smoking campaigns: A theoretical approach. *Health Communication, 15*(3), 349-366. doi:10.1207/s15327027hc1503_6

Hare, T., Camerer, C. F., Knoepfle, D. T., D'Doherty, J. P., & Rangel, A. (2010). Value computations in ventral medial prefrontal cortex during charitable decision making incorporate input from regions involved in social cognition. *The Journal of Neuroscience, 13,* 583-590.

Hare, T. A., O'Doherty, J., Camerer, C. F., Schultz, W., & Rangel, A. (2008). Dissociating the role of the orbitofrontal cortex and the striatum in the computation of goal values and prediction error. *The Journal of Neuroscience, 28,* 5623-5630. Retrieved from http://www.jneurosci.org/cgi/content/abstract/28/22/5623.

Hastings, G., Stead, M., & Webb, J. (2004). Fear appeals in social marketing: Strategic and ethical reasons for concern. *Psychology & Marketing, 21*(11), 961-986. doi:10.1002/mar.20043

Hess, U. (2009). Facial EMG. In E. Harmon-Jones & J. S. Beer (Eds.), *Methods in social neuroscience* (pp. 70-91). New York: The Guilford Press.

Johar, G. V., Maheswaran, D., & Peracchio, L. A. (2006). MAPping the frontiers: Theoretical advances in consumer research on memory, affect, and persuasion. *Journal of Consumer Research, 33*(1), 139-149.

Knutson, B., & Peterson, R. (2005). Neurally constructing expected utility. *Games & Economic Behavior, 52,* 305-315.

Kolb, B., & Whishaw, I. Q. (2009). *Fundamentals of human neuropsy-*

chology (6th ed.). New York, NY: Worth.

Lang, A. (2000). The limited capacity model of mediated message processing. *Journal of Communication, 50*(1), 46-70. doi:10.1111/j.1460-2466.2000.tb02833.x

Langleben, D. D., Loughead, J. W., Ruparel, K., Hakun, J. G., Bush-Winokur, S., Holloway, M. B., . . . Lerman, C. (2009). Reduced prefrontal and temporal processing and recall of high "sensation value" ads. *Neuroimage, 46,* 219-225.

Lau, J. Y., Britton, J. C., Nelson, E. E., Angold, A. A., Ernst, M., Goldwin, M., . . . Pine, D. S. (2011). Distinct neural signatures of threat learning in adolescents and adults. *Proceedings of the National Academy of Science, 108*(11), 4500-4505.

Lesica, N., & Stanley, B. (2004). Encoding of natural scene movies by tonic and burst spikes in the lateral geniculate nucleus. *The Journal of Neuroscience, 24*(47), 10731-10740.

Lim, S. L., O'Doherty, J. P., & Rangel, A. (2011). The decision value computations in the vmPFC and striatum use a relative value code that is guided by visual attention. *Journal of Neuroscience, 31*(37), 13214-13223. doi:10.1523/jneurosci.1246-11.2011

Maddux, J. E., & Rogers, R. W. (1983). Protection motivation and self-efficacy: A revised theory of fear appeals and attitude-change. *Journal of Experimental Social Psychology, 19*(5), 469-479. doi:10.1016/0022-1031(83)90023-9

McGaugh, J. (2000). Memory: A century of consolidation. *Science, 287,* 248-251.

McKay, B., & Kesmodel, D. (2011). Labels give cigarette packs a ghoulish makeover. *The Wall Street Journal, June* Retrieved from http://online.wsj.com/article/SB10001424052702303936704576399320327189158.html.

Mendes, W. B. (2009). Assessing autonomic nervous system activity. In E. Harmon-Jones & J. S. Beer (Eds.), *Methods in social neuroscience* (pp. 118-147). New York, NY: The Guilford Press.

Montgomery, K., & Chester, J. (2008). Interactive food and beverage marketing: Targeting adolescents in the digital age. *Journal of Adolescent Health, 45*, 18-29.

Montgomery, K., & Chester, J. (2011). *Digital food marketing to children and adolescents: Problematic practices and policy interventions.* Retrieved from http://www.ncbi.nlm.nih.gov/pmc/articles/PMC3781010/

Morin, C. (2012). Selection of PSAs Retrieved from http://gme.groupmindexpress.com/salesbrain/?da=f046.

Morris, J., Woo, C., Geason, J., & Kim, J. (2002). The power of affect: Predicting intention. *Journal of Advertising Research, 42*, 7-17.

Murphy, E. R., Illes, J., & Reiner, P. B. (2008). Neuroethics of neuromarketing. *Journal of Consumer Behavior, 7*, 293-302.

Nairn, A. (2009). *Changing the rule of the game: Implicit persuasion and interactive children's marketing.* Retrieved from http://digitalads.org/how-youre-targeted/publications/changing-rules-game-implicit-persuasion-and-interactive-children%E2%80%99s

Nairn, A., & Fine, C. (2008). Who's messing with my mind? The implications of dual-process models for the ethics of advertising to children. *International Journal of Advertising, 27*(3), 447-470.

Noar, S. M. (2006). A 10-year retrospective of research in health mass media campaigns: Where do we go from here? *Journal of Health Communication, 11*(1), 21-42. doi:10.1080/10810730500461059

Palmgreen, P., Donohew, L., Lorch, E. P., Hoyle, R. H., & Stephenson, M. T. (2001). Television campaigns and adolescent marijuana use: Tests of sensation seeking targeting. *American Journal of Public Health, 91*(2), 292-296. doi:10.2105/ajph.91.2.292

Panksepp, J. (1998). *The foundations of human and animal emotions.* New York, NY: Oxford University.

Panksepp, J. (2004). Affective consciousness: Core emotional feelings in animals and humans. *Consciousness and Cognition, 14*, 30-80.

Pechmann, C., Levine, L., Loughlin, S., & Leslie, F. (2005). Impulsive and self-conscious: Adolescents' vulnerability to advertising and promotion. *Journal of Public Policy and Marketing, 24*(2), 202-221.

Petty, R. E., Brinol, P., & Priester, J. R. (2009). Mass media attitude change: Implication of the Elaboration Likelihood Model of Persuasion. In J. Bryant & M. B. Oliver (Eds.), *Media effects: Advances in theory and research* (3rd ed.). New York, NY: Routledge.

Petty, R. E., Cacioppo, J. T., & Heesacker, M. (1981). Effects of rethorical questions on persuasion: A cognitive response analysis. *Journal of Personality and Social Psychology, 40*(3), 432-440. doi:10.1037//0022-3514.40.3.432

Plutchik, R. (1991). *The emotions.* Lanham, MD: University Press of America.

Randolph, W., & Viswanath, K. (2004). Lessons learned from public health mass media campaigns: Marketing health in a crowded media world. *Annual Review of Public Health, 25,* 419-437. doi:10.1146/annurev.publhealth.25.101802.123046

Ravaja, N. (2004). Contributions of psychophysiology to media research: Review and recommendations. *Media Psychology, 6*(2), 193-235.

Reuters. (2012, August 24, 2012). Appeals court blocks graphic warnings on cigarettes. *The New York Times.* Retrieved from http://www.nytimes.com/2012/08/25/business/tobacco-groups-win-ruling-on-graphic-cigarette-warnings.html?_r=1.

Rosenblatt, A., Greenberg, J., Solomon, S., Pyszczynski, T., & Lyon, D. (1989). Evidence of terror management theory: The effects of mortality salience on reactions to those who violate or uphold cultural values. *Journal of Personality and Social Psychology, 57*(4), 681-690.

Rossiter, J. R., Silberstein, R. B., Harris, P. G., & Nield, G. A. (2001). Brain-imaging detection of visual scene encoding in long-term memory for TV commercials. *Journal of Advertising Research, 41,* 13-21.

Rothman, A. J., Martino, S. C., Bedell, B. T., Detweiler, J. B., & Salovey, P. (1999). The systematic influence of gain- and loss-framed messages on interest in and use of different types of health behavior. *Personality and Social Psychology Bulletin, 25*(11), 1355-1369.

doi:10.1177/0146167299259003

Strasburger, V. C. (2009). Why do adolescent health researchers ignore the impact of the media? *Journal of Adolescent Health, 44*, 203-205.

Strasburger, V. C., Jordan, A. B., & Donnerstein, E. (2009). Health effects of media on children and adolescents. *Pediatrics, 125*(4), 756-767.

Sutfin, E. L., Szykman, L. R., & Moore, M. C. (2008). Adolescents' responses to anti-tobacco advertising: Exploring the role of adolescents' smoking status and advertisement theme. *Journal of Health Communication, 13*(5), 480-500. doi:10.1080/10810730802198961

Tamietto, M., & de Gelder, B. (2010, September). Neural bases of the non-conscious perception of emotional signals. *Nature Reviews Neuroscience*, 1-13.

Tusche, A., Bode, S., & Haynes, J. D. (2010). Neural responses to unattended products predict later consumer choices. *Journal of Neuroscience, 30*(23), 8024-8031.

Walsh, D., & Gentile, D. A. (2003). Slipping under the radar: Advertising and the mind. In L.R.I. Obot (Ed.), *Drinking it in: Alcohol and yound people*. Geneva, Switzerland: World Health Organization.

Wang, A., Ruparel, K. Loughead, J. W., Strasser, A. A., Blady, S. J., Lynch, K. G., . . . Langleben, D. D. (2013). Content matters: Neuroimaging investigation of brain and behavioral impact of televised anti-tobacco public service announcements. *The Journal of Neuroscience, 33*(17), 7420-7247.

WHO. (2012). Tobacco fact sheet: Picture warnings work. Retrieved from http://www.who.int/mediacentre/factsheets/fs339/en/index.html.

Witte, K., & Allen, M. (2000). A meta-analysis of fear appeals: Implications for effective public health campaigns. *Health Education & Behavior, 27*(5), 591-615. doi:10.1177/109019810002700506

About the Author

With over 30 years of consumer research experience, Christophe Morin, PhD is passionate about understanding and predicting consumer behavior using media psychology and neuroscience. Christophe has held numerous executive positions during his career. Prior to founding SalesBrain, he was Chief Marketing Officer of rStar Networks, a public company that developed the largest private network ever deployed in U.S. schools. Christophe has received multiple awards during his career. In 2011 and 2013, he received prestigious speaking awards from Vistage International. In 2011 and 2014, he received Great Mind Research Awards from the Advertising Research Foundation (ARF).

Christophe holds a BA in marketing, an MBA from Bowling Green State University, and an MA and a PhD in media psychology from Fielding Graduate University. He is an adjunct faculty member at Fielding Graduate University, where he teaches several courses he designed called "The Psychology of Neuromarketing" and "Introduction to Consumer Neuroscience." He is also the lead faculty member for an innovative postgraduate program launched in 2015 entitled "Certificate in Media Psychology With an Emphasis in Media Neuroscience." Christophe has been a board member of the Neuromarketing Science and Business Association (NMSBA) since it was founded in 2012 and is leading efforts in setting ethics and scientific standards used by its members worldwide.

Publications

Lin, P., Grewal N., Morin, C., Johnson, W., Zak, P. (2013). Oxytocin increases the influence of public service advertisements. *PLoS ONE, 8*(2), e56934. doi:10.1371/journal.pone.0056934

Morin, C. (2011) Neuromarketing: The new science of consumer behavior. *Society, 48*(2), 131-135.

Morin, C. (2014). *The neurophysiological effect of emotional ads on the brains of late adolescents and young adults.* A dissertation submitted for the degree of Doctor in Philosophy in Psychology with an emphasis in Media Psychology.

Morin, C. & Renvoise, P. (2007) Neuromarketing: *Understanding the buy buttons in your customer's brain.* Nashville, TN: Thomas Nelson.

IF WE BUILD IT, WILL SHE COME? A CROSS-CULTURAL STUDY OF PSYCHOLOGICAL FACTORS AFFECTING WOMEN'S MOBILE PHONE USE

Deirdre Bradley, MSc, U.C. Davis; PhD,
Fielding Graduate University, USA

Abstract: A behavioral study was conducted to assess the importance of three psychological factors—attitude, perceived norm, and perceived ability—in forming a woman's intention to use mobile technology, specifically mobile business apps (e.g., banking, e-commerce). The study also tested whether the significance of these factors varied across cultures, analyzing data collected from three culturally diverse countries in the Asia-Pacific region: Indonesia; South Korea; and New Zealand. The proposed model, based on the theory of reasoned action,[1] was highly significant in predicting intention to use the apps, with the attitude construct consistently significant across all cultures. Beliefs around improved efficiency and convenience were most important in forming attitude. The perceived norm and control constructs were significant in the overall model but not for each culture. However, the belief that mobile apps allow a woman to independently control her own finances was highly significant across all three countries. The results suggest that the success of mobile-for-development (M4D) projects aimed at increasing women's use of business apps would be enhanced if their promotional messaging emphasized three areas: attitude formation highlighting convenience and efficiency; personal control and the independence that comes with managing one's own finances; and additional specific beliefs identified for each culture.

Keywords: women's empowerment, mobile pay, mobile apps, mobile-for-development, M4D, gender empowerment, reasoned action theory

Introduction

Are smartphones the ultimate answer to closing the digital gender divide? Many of those working to improve the lives of women in developing countries believe this is the case.

Mobile phones are being touted as the best tool to motivate women to start businesses, to access public services, and to make their voices heard by their governments (m-government). These are behaviors that do not directly relate to social activities, the prevalent way women currently use mobile phones. In addition, they require users to interact with strangers and place trust in applications built by unknown people—predominantly male—that often reflect unfamiliar cultural mores. To realize the potential that smartphones and their apps represent, we need to better understand the intrinsic factors that women use in determining whether to adopt this technology.

Research Importance

In the past decade, we have seen the launch and initial success of Mobile-for-Development (M4D) projects that are making a real difference in empowering women globally. The World Bank has launched a Land Portal for women to register land boundaries and ownership so that, in the event a husband dies or deserts his family, their rights to the land are not lost (World Bank, 2013). A live birth registration mobile program was successfully launched in Tanzania in 2014 (UNICEF, 2014; 2002). Registering a birth entitles these children to the full rights of citizenship (voting, finding jobs, opening bank accounts), while also making them less vulnerable to child trafficking. The Manobi Development Foundation has launched a Small Farmer's Access to Market Info system, in which women with little money or education are able to use a mobile pay-phone business run by community women to obtain vital information for selling their crops (Manobi, n.d.). The use of mobile technology not only reduces the cost of delivering development projects in many cases (GSMA, 2015), but holds great potential for building the incomes of the target recipients, especially underserved women.

Background

Nearly two-thirds of the world's population (over four billion people) still has no regular access to the Internet, and 90% of those households are in the developing world. As a region, Europe has the highest Internet adoption (77%) while Africa has the lowest (7%).[2] In both developed and developing countries, more men than women use the Internet, but the gap is significantly smaller in the industrial world—2% in developed countries vs. 16% in less developed countries (ITU, 2012a).

Figure 1. Percent penetration of smartphone use worldwide
(data from the ICT Indicator Database, 2013)

The smartphone, which can provide Internet access to underserved populations, holds great promise for helping to close this gap. In 2013, the number of mobile-cellular subscriptions nearly matched the global population, with more than half of these in the Asia-Pacific region. However, women are 21% less likely to own a mobile phone on average, a number that soars to almost 45% in sub-Saharan Africa and 38% in South Asia (GSMA, 2015, 2010; Intel, 2012). The good news is that this gender gap is closing. It is projected that about two out of every three new phone subscriptions in 2014 will prove to be by women, representing 600 million of 900 million new subscribers and US$29 billion to ICT companies, a win-win proposition (GSMA, 2015).

From the developed world, we know that women were slower to adopt Internet technology than men (ITU, 2011; Bimber, 2000), that they use it differently (ITU-UNESCO, 2013; Zhou & Xu, 2007), and that they regard it as a useful tool but one to which they cannot easily relate (Baruch,

2014). These results hint that psychological factors may present significant barriers to mobile adoption that will first need to be identified, then overcome. This study was designed to investigate these potential factors.

Technological Innovation

Transitions from era to era are often marked by radical social change caused by the development of disruptive technology and, as with previous technological revolutions, our current digital era has also produced drastic societal changes. Within just the past few decades, the transition of the Internet from a military and scientific networking tool to a public resource has provided us with unprecedented access to communication and information, and our lives have been inexorably changed. Technology has also evolved to become personal—our appliances are programmed to our lifestyles, the Web displays information relevant to our detected tastes, and our phones provide access to applications once available only on room-sized mainframes or desktop computers.

While the Internet has been extensively adopted across industrialized societies, the cost of building infrastructure, especially in more remote areas, has meant lack of access for less-developed countries, creating a "digital divide" (Prasad, 2012; Ruth, 2012). However, recent research has shown that developing nations are "leapfrogging" the broadband stage and moving straight to mobile, allowing for the rapid adoption of the new technology, and effectively closing the divide faster than anyone could anticipate prior to the advent of mobile information and communications technologies or ICT (ITU, 2013).[3]

The Gender Gap in Technology

The impact of this rapid evolution in technology on people and whether they choose to interact with it continues to engender numerous studies across multiple disciplines, especially the related fields of sociology, anthropology, and psychology. However, most of the research on technology design and adoption has focused on acceptance by men, due in part to the absence of women in IT departments in universities or corporations (GSMA, 2010). Research in those early years labeled women as inherently "technophobic," a label that stuck for decades (Brosnan, 2002), but has since been largely dismissed.

While the reasons for women lagging in adoption of IT are still not well understood, researchers have speculated that the design of the technology itself and its corresponding software—how they look, feel, and operate—is dominated by a male perspective (Oleksy, Just, & Zapedowska-Kling, 2012; Bimber, 2000). A United Nations report on gender issues in ICT policy (Hafkin, 2002) highlighted the fact that the ICT sector is one of the last areas to adopt a gender perspective, with considerable evidence to support the allegation that policymaking in tech fields ignores gender issues. When ICT studies did include women, the results demonstrated a clear "gender gap"—women were not embracing technology at the same rate as men.

Family or community social norms may also hinder women from going out in public to use cybercafés, or there may be a gender bias around investing more resources in sons than daughters, reserving technology and other tools of education for males (Hafkin, 2002). Non-Internet users were six times more likely to cite family opposition in a 2012 Intel report; an impact of cultural norms on Internet use was also confirmed. When compared to awareness or access, gender roles were a less significant factor for use in Mexico and Uganda, while the opposite was true in India and Egypt (Intel, 2012). And while teenagers and young women may be more aware of the Internet and its uses, they also report greater opposition from their families due to concerns over safety or exposure to pornography. In some countries such as Egypt where this is a significant factor, there have been calls to provide websites designed for, and dedicated to, women's use only (Gillwald, 2012). There is even an international group dedicated to this concept—the Feminist Approach to Technology, or FAT (Intel, 2012).

What about intrinsic factors? The results of an early email study by Gefen and Straub (1997) found that women and men differ in their perceptions, but not their use, of email. A number of studies found that men were more strongly influenced by perceived usefulness and performance, while women found ease of use and subjective norm (perceived social pressure) were more important factors (Lichtenstein & Williamson, 2006; Van Slyke et al., 2002; Venkatesh & Morris, 2000; Gefen & Straub, 1997). Significantly, these studies also found that the effect of subjective norm diminished over time, which helps to explain why the gender gap continues to close. The unified theory of acceptance and use of technology (UTAUT), which merges a number of separate theories into one overall model, proposed that gender would be a significant factor in mitigating the importance of performance and effort expectancy, as well as social influence (Venkatesh, Morris, Davis, & Davis, 2003). Over time, however, these gender differences have been shown to narrow as technology diffusion continues. No gender differences in the determinants of intention to adopt were found in computer use studies in universities by Wong, Teo, and Russo (2012) and Marchewka, Liu, and Kostiwa (2007). A recent study on adoption of mobile payment technology in Spain found that subjective norm was the most significant factor in intention to use for both genders, whereas perceived ease of use had a significant influence on intention to use only for men, a complete reversal of earlier study findings cited above. Thus, overall, study results do not provide a clear picture.

In some geographic regions, and for certain uses, women are eager consumers of ICT. Women outnumber men in their use of blogs and social applications such as Facebook and Pinterest (Stavrositu & Sundar, 2012; Clifford, 2014). In contrast, men predominantly use Web apps for entertainment and gaming (Forrester, 2010). There is also evidence that women broaden their use over time (Intel, 2012). Recent large studies of mobile technology such as the one produced by Intel (2012) have shown that disparities in gender use of ICT ranges from nearly zero in regions such as North and South America, to sizable disparities of nearly 60% in parts of South Asia and Africa. This study also found that high proportions of female nonusers of the Internet in Egypt and India stated that they were not "interested" in using the Internet.

The question arises: Why aren't they interested? Is it due to lack of knowledge of what the Internet can provide them? Misconceptions about the danger of online interactions? Cultural dictates? A generic response to end the interview? Or is there something inherent in how women perceive the Internet?

Factors Affecting ICT Adoption by Women

Technology adoption by women reflects a complex set of physical, economic, cultural, and psychological barriers, often engendered by lack of income, education, access, time, and independent control (Huyer & Sikoska, 2003). From a development perspective, governments, NGOs, and private foundations seek to better understand and advance progress on this issue. As two-thirds of the world's women are not yet using ICT (representing the largest potential market for cellular providers), corporations are also playing a significant role in working to overcome barriers in their adoption of mobile technology, providing free handsets, subsidized call plans, and targeted marketing and education campaigns (GSMA, 2010). In this way, the organizations are addressing socioeconomic barriers to adoption—lack of access to the technology due to cost, time constraints due to family responsibilities, and lack of information about the uses and benefits of the technology. A 2008 study conducted across sub-Saharan countries found that, in 11 of the 15 countries surveyed, men were more likely to know what the Internet was, often in significantly greater numbers (Intel, 2012). It is common for people to learn how to use the Internet in school and at work, but in developing countries girls often do not attend school and women predominantly work in their homes and fields, so these educational opportunities are not available to them. The issue is not restricted to rural areas, or to lower levels of income or education (Gillwald, 2012). A report on women and Web use found that awareness of the Internet was not generally correlated with income, that higher income nonusers were equally as likely as lower income nonusers to respond that they "didn't need" or "weren't interested" in the technology (Intel, 2012). Twenty percent of the respondents—urban, professional women—stated that they weren't familiar with, or comfortable with, the technology. The same study also found that 37% of all female nonusers surveyed cited discomfort with the technology as a reason. The challenges of implementing projects in rural areas, where women have had little exposure to technology, will prove to be even more complex.

We therefore need to better understand the when, why, and how women use ICT in order to continue designing and implementing successful social and economic development projects aimed at empowering women. What is the most effective way to educate women on the existence of these technologies and how they operate? What is the best way to alleviate fears or misconceptions women have about using online applications? If women are more affected by perceived effort in their adoption decisions, how can we present the technology in order to minimize this effect? What types of applications should we build, and how should we design them to foster use? Finally, how are the answers to these questions impacted by culture and individual psyche?

Theories Related to Technology Adoption Behavior

Adoption of a new technology is a decision; the user chooses to engage with the new product or application or not. The factors that go into making that decision, and the relative importance of each factor, are a much more complex issue, as they ultimately rely on understanding and predicting human behavior.

Over time, a multitude of theories and models have emerged to explain general principles of motivation and behavior. Prominent among them are social cognitive theory (Bandura, 2001), the social identity approach (Tajfel & Turner, 1986), and reasoned action theory (Fishbein, 1979). Variations of these models have been developed to better understand the drivers of particular behaviors—for example consumer purchasing decisions (Brewer, 1994; Ha, 1998); AIDS prevention (Fisher, Fisher, & Rye, 1995); drug, alcohol, and gambling education (Thrasher, Andrew, & Mahony, 2011; Sharma & Kanekar, 2007); and domestic violence prevention (Nabi, Southwell, & Hornik, 2002).

For this study of the relative importance of psychological factors in a woman's decision to engage with non-social mobile applications, the tenets of these theories, along with important concepts from the fields of cross-cultural and gender psychology, were used to inform the analysis.

The primary theory used to create the behavioral model for the analysis is the reasoned action approach (the theory of reasoned action and the theory of planned behavior).

Reasoned Action Approach (RAA/TRA/TPB)

The late 1960s and 1970s engendered a wealth of research into the role of cognition on behavior. Among the models generated was the theory of reasoned action (TRA), which was developed by Marvin Fishbein in 1979 to predict social behavior based on perceived beliefs and intention to act (Fishbein, 1979). This model has been widely adapted and used to predict behavior across a number of disciplines including technology adoption (e.g., the technology adoption model).

The TRA is comprised of sets of beliefs that form two constructs: behavioral beliefs (benefit/cost of the action) form the construct "attitude," and normative beliefs (approval/disapproval of the social circle) form the construct "perceived norm." Attitude refers to a person's belief in whether performing a certain behavior will be a positive or negative experience. Perceived norm reflects a person's belief in whether those people or groups important in her or his life would approve or disapprove of the behavior. Behavioral control is taken as volitional. In addition to these components, the model acknowledges the influence that background factors such as education, values, age, and so forth can have on behavior.

Ajzen (1991) revised the TRA model to replace volitional control with a third construct—perceived behavioral control—shaped by control beliefs. These beliefs refer to personal or environmental factors that will either promote or inhibit the behavior (efficacy). When these three elements are combined, they lead to an overall intention to act. This variation, called the theory of planned behavior (TPB), recognizes that not all factors are under the control of the participant; outside factors may intervene to prevent the behavior (action) from actually taking place. In the context of mobile adoption, the external aspect of "actual control," which is not part of the intention process, reflects factors such as lack of access to the phones, their cost, and lack of information about their use. It is these factors that most development and ICT organizations have targeted to eliminate as a barrier to adoption, with increasing success (ITU, 2012). The third iteration of the TRA theory, the reasoned action approach, was proposed by both Fishbein and Ajzen to merge the two earlier theory versions. As with the TPB, the theory is comprised of three constructs: attitudes; perceived (subjective) norms; and control beliefs (Figure 2), and recognizes the potential effect of background factors (Fishbein & Ajzen, 2010).

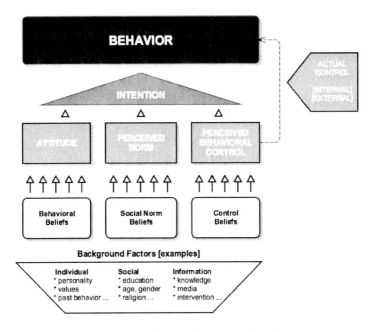

Figure 2. Illustration depicting the reasoned action approach (based on Ajzen, 1991).[4]

Generally, the greater the positive sum of these constructs, the more probable it is that the individual will enact the behavior. The relative importance an individual will place on each of these constructs is expected to vary with the target behavior and with the population (culture) involved (Fishbein & Ajzen, 2010).

This model provides a robust framework for analyzing a woman's decision to adopt mobile technology, as the three constructs—behavioral, normative, and control beliefs—will reflect both individual difference and cultural influence in forming intention.

Research Questions and Analytical Model

This research project was designed to examine the relative importance of behavioral, normative, and control beliefs on women's intention to use business-related mobile applications. For the purposes of this study, business apps are defined as those used to conduct financial transactions such as online banking, e-commerce, and interacting with government services, and exclude apps focused on personal or social interactions. By identifying and analyzing those factors that influence the decision of women from diverse cultures to adopt mobile technology, development agencies and corporations committed to empowering women through access to mobile technologies will be aided in designing and implementing their campaigns more effectively.

The reasoned action approach (RAA) provided the framework for this analysis. The RAA relies on the principle that intention to act is a strong predictor of later actual behavior. There are two main aspects of the RAA design: constructs and beliefs. The three constructs of attitude, social norm, and perceived behavioral control are evaluated for their relative contribution in explaining the remaining construct, intention to act. Sets of beliefs provide insight into how the first three constructs are formed. Thus, within the RAA model, the explanatory constructs form intention, while the beliefs form the constructs. Within the model, it is possible for any of the constructs (and, indirectly, their related beliefs) to be statistically insignificant in explaining intention; the relative importance of each has been shown to vary with the target behavior being examined, and the population being studied (Ajzen, 2002, 1991).

For this study, the model was used to design and formulate the questions that would gather data to analyze the following:

□ How do the three constructs differ in significance when examined in the context of intention to adopt mobile business applications (e.g., is attitude more strongly correlated with intent than perceived control)?

☐   Does the relative significance of each of the three constructs vary by culture?

The corresponding research hypotheses are:

H1: The three model constructs—attitude, social norm, and perceived control—will each be significant in explaining intention to enact the target behavior.

H2: The relative significance of each belief construct will vary by culture.

Methodology

Defining the Behavior

Within the RAA, there are four aspects that define a behavior: the action; the target at which the action is directed; the context of the action; and the time at which the action occurs. Of these four, only the action itself needs to be clearly defined; the other elements can be generalized (Fishbein & Ajzen, 2010).

Target Behavior for This Study

The behavior defined for this study is the use (*action*) by women of business applications (*target*) on mobile phones (*context*) at any time (*time*).

Survey Questions

Following the prescripts of using the RAA to study behavioral intention, a pilot study was conducted to define the set of behavioral beliefs and direct measures of attitude, perceived norm, and perceived behavioral control (Fishbein & Ajzen 2010). A series of 34 questions was then formulated based on the pilot study responses in order to assess each of the theory's four constructs. In addition to the measures of attitudes and beliefs, the survey also included 16 socio-demographic questions, which are termed *background factors* in the RAA. The format of the questions and answers followed the United Nations/ITU guidelines for data collection on ICT studies (ITU, 2014).

Research Population

For the standard study, the only two participant requirements were (a) female gender, and (b) age 18 years or older. The participants may or may not have had prior experience with mobile phones, as RAA theory dictates that past experience is not a reliable factor in predicting future behavior (Fishbein & Ajzen, 2010).

The survey was conducted across three countries in the Asia-Pacific region: South Korea; Indonesia; and New Zealand. There were multiple considerations in the selection of these three countries. One primary consideration was how they were classified by culture according to two important theories: Schwartz' transnational cultural groupings by values (Schwartz, Montgomery, & Briones, 2006; Schwartz, 1999), which is an extension of Hofstede's cultural dimensions theory (1980). Schwartz classified subjects according to seven values types, based on shared history, geographical proximity, religion, and development stage. The three countries under focus for this study have distinctly different histories, major religions, development stages (measured using the GINI index), and geographical locations. As Figure 5 depicts, each country falls into a different Schwartz classification: New Zealand (*English speaking*); Indonesia (*South Asia*); South Korea (*Confucian influenced*).

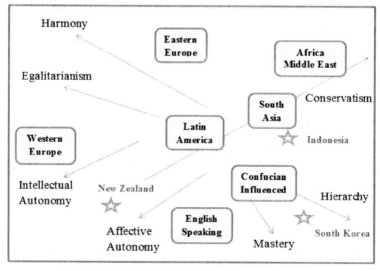

Figure 5. Transnational cultural groupings
(based on Schwartz et al., 2006)

In Hofstede's seminal studies on culture and organizations (1991, 1980), countries were assigned to cultural groups according to four constructs:

power distance; individualism/collectivism; masculinity/femininity; and uncertainty avoidance. Each of the three focus countries varies across these four dimensions, as seen in Figure 6.

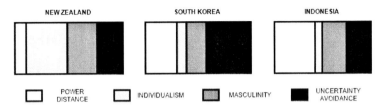

Figure 6. Research countries classified according to Hofstede (1991)

The ITU, in partnership with the United Nations, produces a series of annual reports that document how rapidly ICT is being adopted globally (2013, 2012a,b). In 2013, the corresponding ICT Development Index (IDI) ranked South Korea as #1 in the world, New Zealand as #16, and Indonesia as #97. Therefore, the data portray South Korea as having a population with ready access to the Internet on their phones; there is a mid-range percentage for the population of New Zealand, and a low percentage for Indonesia, indicating that mobile phones for that population are still predominantly using SMS technology (ITU, 2013).

Unfortunately, data collected by gender remain sparse in most ICT data collection. The closest statistic obtainable is Internet use by gender (ITU, 2012a). The data for the target countries are (male vs. female, year data collected): South Korea (88.1% vs. 80.0%, 2012); New Zealand (80.6% vs.78.4%, 2011), and Indonesia (11.1%, 8.7%, 2010). While this provides some insight into male vs. female technology adoption, research data show that you cannot extrapolate mobile phone use from Internet use. However, the data do consistently show that mobile use exceeds Internet use (ITU, 2013).

The World Economic Forum publishes a global gender gap index each year, based on a number of categories such as economic participation and opportunity, education and technology, and political empowerment. For the three study countries, the values for the equality score (0.000 = full inequality-1.000 = full equality) and rank (# out of 136 countries) were: Indonesia (score = 0.661, rank = 95); South Korea (score = 0.635, rank =

111); New Zealand (score = 0.780, rank = 7) (World Economic Forum, 2013). It is interesting to note the dichotomy of South Korea, which ranks as #1 for ICT globally, but ranks low for gender equality.

Survey Administration

The research survey was administered through the online survey tool provided by Qualtrics (http://www.qualtrics.com). The company has extensive partnerships around the world that allowed the survey to be administered and tracked in the target countries. The company's policy follows IRB regulations for complete anonymity of responses. The survey was translated and back-translated into the corresponding native languages for South Korea and Indonesia, a standard process for cross-cultural research protocols (Hui & Triandis, 1985).

Sample Size

Sample size was determined using the guidelines recommended for an RAA analysis—a minimum of 150 responses, or 3–5 respondents for each variable (Fishbein & Ajzen, 2010); for this study, that corresponded to a sample size of 99–165. To provide a buffer for surveys with incomplete data, the instrument was distributed to a total of 252 respondents, 84 in each of the three countries.

Statistical Analysis

Model Assessment

According to the guidelines presented by Fishbein and Ajzen (2010) and Fornell and Larcker (1981), the statistical analysis of the model generally has two phases: examining the measurement model to confirm the reliability and validity of the constructs and belief sets using Cronbach's alpha; and analyzing the structural model to assess the strength and direction of the constructs' relationships using a principal components analysis. This process was followed using the statistical program SPSS v22 to conduct the reliability and validity calculations for the constructs and belief sets. Once the model was assessed, the survey data were analyzed to determine the validity of the two study hypotheses. First, multiple regressions were run on the data, with *intention* as the dependent variable and the three constructs as the independent variables, to test the first hypothesis. Then additional regression analyses were run by country to assess the second hypothesis—that the relative importance of each construct in terms of intention would differ by country. Appropriate analyses of the belief sets were run to determine their significance in explaining each of the constructs, overall and by county.

Data Assessment

Lack of response was not an issue for this survey, as very few questions had any missing data, and the number of completed surveys surpassed the statistical requirement for 165 surveys. As the mean is used for each construct, having a blank entry did not impact the value.

Results

Statistical Analysis: H1

Constructs. A multiple regression analysis was run to determine the relative importance of the three predictors—attitude, social norm, and perceived control—in determining intention to enact the target behavior, that is, the use of mobile business apps across all three countries. The resultant model was: Intention = -1.086 + .815 (Attitude) + .227 (Perceived Norm) + .180 (Perceived Control)

The model is highly significant at the 1% level, $F(3,246) = 424.900$, $p<.001$, and explains about 84% of the variance in intention, $R^2 = .838$.

Assumptions needed to use this form of analysis were also tested; residuals were shown to be uncorrelated (Durbin-Watson statistic of 1.9), and there was no detectable multicollinearity among the constructs (tolerance above 0.1; VIF below 10). Casewise diagnostics revealed no significant outliers.

Direct Measures. All attitude direct measure items were highly significant, with two measures contributing approximately twice the level of the other three measures: "using mobile business apps . . . allows me to accomplish my tasks faster" and "I can benefit from using mobile business apps." Three of the four social norm direct measures were highly significant in explaining the variance within intention: "Most people who are important to me think I should use mobile business applications"; "Most people whose opinions I value would approve of my using mobile business applications"; "Most people like me use business apps on their phone." Three of the four behavioral control direct measures were highly significant: two capacity measures, "I am confident that, if I wanted to, I could use business apps on my mobile phone," and "I have the resources needed to use mobile business applications;" and one autonomy measure, "Whether I use mobile business apps is completely under my control."

Belief Sets. A regression analysis was run on each belief set to determine their statistical significance in explaining the variance in the corresponding construct. Each belief *group* was found statistically significant in explaining the variance in the related construct, but each belief *statement* within the group was not individually significant.

Statistical Analysis: H2

Constructs. The second hypothesis asserts that the significance of each construct in explaining behavioral intention would vary by country. A multiple regression analysis was run separately on each country's data to determine the relative importance of the three predictors. Assumptions needed to use this form of analysis were also tested, as described earlier.

Indonesia. The results obtained were $F(3,80) = 74.910$, $p < .001$; $R^2 = .737$. Therefore, the Indonesia overall model is statistically highly significant and explains approximately 74% of the variance in intention for this country. The relative importance of each construct was also tested, and each was highly significant at $p < .001$. The regression model for Indonesia is Intention = 0.272 + 0.388(Attitude) + 0.259(Social Norm) + 0.338 (Perceived Control).

South Korea. The results obtained were $F(3,79) = 126.554$, $p < .001$; $R^2 = .828$. Therefore, the South Korean model is highly significant and explains approximately 83% of the variance in intention for this country. The relative importance of each construct was: attitude and perceived control were highly significant at $p < .001$. Social norm did not achieve statistical significance at a 95% confidence level. The regression model for South Korea is Intention = -0.699 + 0.736(Attitude) +0.319 (Perceived Control).

New Zealand. The results obtained were $F(3,79) = 115.359, p < .001; R^2 = .814$. Therefore, the New Zealand model is highly significant and explains approximately 81% of the variance in intention for this country. The relative importance of each construct in explaining intention was that all three constructs were significant, but at different levels: attitude, $p < .001$; social norm, $p = .028$; perceived control, $p = .077$. Using a 95% confidence level eliminates the perceived control construct from this country's model. The resultant model is Intention = -1.757 + 0.931 (Attitude) + 0.240 (Social Norm).

The unstandardized regression coefficients for each country show that, for Indonesia, each construct contributes nearly equally to explaining intention, while for South Korea attitude is about twice as important as perceived control, and for New Zealand attitude is about four times as important as social norm.

Comparison of construct means by country. To gain further insight into how the behavioral model applies to the three countries, a comparison of the construct means per culture was generated, using Likert scales coded or reverse-coded to result in an overall positive score on a scale from 1 (least positive) to 7 (most positive). Across all three constructs, Indonesia exhibited the highest positive mean value, followed by South Korea, then New Zealand. All values were determined to be statistically different.

Belief sets. As with the overall model, a regression analysis was run on each country's belief sets to determine statistical significance. Each belief *set* was found statistically significant, but each belief *item* was not individually significant.

Comparison of belief set means by country. As with the constructs, a comparison of the belief set means for each culture was generated to inform the overall results. Across all three construct belief sets, Indonesia consistently exhibited the most positive attitude towards the behavior, and New Zealand consistently exhibited the lowest positive values. This confirms the concept that these beliefs provide insight into the mental formation of the constructs, and confirm the structure of this RAA model.

Discussion

This study examined the intention of women to enact a particular behavior—using business-based mobile applications. According to the RAA model used in this study, attitude is the most important construct in predicting behavioral intention (Fishbein & Ajzen, 2010). This study's results are in agreement. For the overall model, a one-unit change in attitude effected about three times the change in intention compared to social norm, and nearly six times the change due to perceived control in this model.

The data also demonstrate that the importance of each construct in determining intention is significantly different among the three countries. All three belief sets—behavioral, normative, and perceived control—proved to be statistically significant at the highest level. Therefore, the goodness of fit for the model is again confirmed.

By country, the data show that Indonesia exhibited the strongest agreement responses to all three constructs and belief sets, and therefore presented the strongest overall positive attitude towards intention to use mobile business apps. According to a 2014 GSMA/Qualcomm report, Indonesian women look favorably upon using mobile phones for business, so the findings of this research are supportive (Qualcomm, 2014). This is in contrast to studies on Internet or mobile use in other culturally conservative countries (Intel, 2012). While Indonesia, like other Islamic countries, may be culturally conservative (Schwartz et al., 2013), according to the Global Gender Gap Report for 2013 Indonesian women fare better than in many other culturally conservative cultures (e.g., Indonesia ranks 95/136; Pakistan ranks 135/136). South Korea exhibited the second highest level of positive response, followed by New Zealand.

Why, despite the availability of the technology and no identified cultural barriers, are women in an economically advantaged country still at what appears to be "early adopters" to "early majority" stages, according to Rogers' (1995) theory of technology adoption? In looking to explain both the comparative lack of current mobile use and the lowest positive attitude towards the technology for business use, one factor could be age. An analysis of the average age of the respondents by country showed that

Indonesia had the overall youngest respondents, while New Zealand had the oldest. South Korea's average age was closer to New Zealand's than Indonesia's. The age data obtained in the study do, in fact, echo the average female age in each country's population. A Spearman correlation run on age and intention showed a weak negative correlation that was nonetheless statistically significant.

Another possible reason, which I believe is an important factor, is that women in South Korea and New Zealand have options for conducting their own business that may not be open to, or easily accessed by, women in Indonesia. Thus, for Indonesian women mobile technology may represent a new form of independence not readily available otherwise. This could also help to explain the much higher positive attitude towards use of mobile business apps exhibited by Indonesian women. This is an important topic for future research. It would also be interesting to see whether men in New Zealand exhibit a similar percentage of mobile use to women, in order to provide insight into whether this low percentage is based more in gender or in culture.

Conclusion

In accordance with the reasoned action approach, this study successfully demonstrated that attitude, and the underlying beliefs that form attitude, are most important in a woman's decision to enact the target behavior of using mobile business apps. The study also made clear that the beliefs underlying the construct varied in significance by country. For those organizations hoping to increase mobile adoption, it will be important to correctly identify those beliefs and then craft messages and training that address them.

Previous studies on technology adoption that employed the related TAM model generally found men relied more heavily on the technology's performance when considering use, while women were more influenced by perceived effort (Lichtenstein & Williamson, 2006; Van Slyke et al., 2002). The direct measure that assessed perceived ease of use within this study was highly significant in explaining variance, in agreement with this body of literature. This should then be emphasized when designing mobile business applications and promoting their use.

Among social norm beliefs, those related to someone important to the respondent already enacting the behavior were shown to be significant, while those related to approval or disapproval by people important to the respondent were not. By country, the only norm belief that was significant across all three was "people like me are likely to use mobile business applications." Thus, messaging to promote adoption should focus on presenting images and information on people "like them" (i.e., like the target population) using the technology. Social norm effects were lower for the countries that had been exposed to mobile technology longer, echoing the results of an earlier study by Venkatesh and Morris (2000). This suggests that agencies might want to change their marketing approaches over time, with a higher emphasis on social norm at the earlier phases of the project.

With respect to perceived control, across all three countries the most significant belief was women's ability to control their own finances, and the most significant direct measure of control was that respondents were confident that they could use the business apps. Combining these two beliefs—the capability to use the apps and the ability to independently control their finances—would make a powerful message to promote adoption.

In summary, the results of the survey are encouraging, as women from very culturally diverse countries do seem to be embracing mobile business, but the standout finding is Indonesia's very positive attitude towards using mobile business applications. A more in-depth study of this unique country, and how women in a culturally conservative culture are nonetheless venturing into mobile banking and e-commerce, could bring real insights that might be applied to culturally similar countries that are lagging behind.

Endnotes

[1] The theory of reasoned action was developed by Martin Fishbein in 1979. A variation of the model developed by Icek Ajzen in 1991, the theory of planned behavior, no longer assumed volitional control over the target behavior and added the construct of perceived behavioral control. A joint

publication in 2010 by Fishbein and Ajzen merged the jointly developed theory, renaming it the reasoned action approach.

[2] The good news is that Africa exhibited the highest rate of growth for Internet penetration between 2009 and 2013, followed by Asia/Pacific, the Arab States, and the CIS (ITU, 2013).

[3] The term "digital divide" was originally used in 1997 (Katz & Aspden) to describe inequities in Internet access across the United States. It has since taken on a broader meaning to include access to all forms of ICT as well as the lack of skills, education, and cultural freedom to utilize this technology.

[4] The original diagram on which this figure is based is the copyright of Icek Ajzen; permission is granted for use for non-commercial purposes (http://people.umass.edu/aizen/tpb.diag.html).

[5] GINI is a coefficient that represents the amount of income inequality within a country; a low number indicates a more equal distribution.

References

Ajzen, I. (1991). The theory of planned behavior. *Organizational Behavior and Human Decision Processes, 50*(2), 179-211.

Ajzen, I. (2002). Perceived behavioral control, self-efficacy, locus of control, and the theory of planned behavior. *Journal of Applied Social Psychology, 32*(4), 665-683.

Bandura, A. (2001). Social cognitive theory: An agentic perspective. *Annual Review of Psychology, 52*(1), 1-26.

Baruch, R. (2014). Women and information technology: How do female students of education perceive information technology, and what is their approach to it? *Journal of International Women's Studies, 15*(1), 190-214.

Bimber, B. (2000). Measuring the gender gap on the Internet. *Social Science Quarterly, 81*(3), 868-876.

Brewer, K. (1994). Exploring cultural differences in consumer decision making: Chinese consumers in Montreal. *Advances in Consumer Research, 21*, 318-322.

Brosnan, M. (2002). *Technophobia: The psychological impact of informa-tion technology.* London, UK: Routledge.

Clifford, C. (2014). Women dominate every social media network- except one. *Entrepreneur Magazine.* Retrieved from http://www.entre-preneur.com/article/231970

Fishbein, M. (1979). A theory of reasoned action: Some applications and implications. *Nebraska Symposium on Motivation, 27,* 65-116.

Fishbein, M., & Ajzen, I. (2010). *Predicting and changing behavior: The reasoned action approach.* New York, NY: Taylor & Francis.

Fisher, W. A., Fisher, J. D., & Rye, B. J. (1995). Understanding and pro-moting AIDS-preventive behavior: Insights from the theory of reasoned action. *Health Psychology, 14*(3), 255-264.

Fornell, C., & Larcker, D. F. (1981). Evaluating structural equation mod-els with unobservable variables and measurement error. *Journal of Marketing Research, 18,* 39-50.

Forrester Research Group. (2010). *North American Technographics Benchmark Survey.*

Gefen, D., & Straub, D. (1997). Gender differences in the perception and use of e-mail: An extension to the technology acceptance model. *MIS Quarterly,* 389-400.

Gillwald, A. (2012). Understanding broadband demand in Africa: Internet going mobile. ResearchICT Africa. Retrieved from http://www.researchictafrica.net/docs/Gillwald%20CITI%20Zambia%20Broadband%202012.pdf

GSMA. (2015). *Bridging the gender gap: Mobile access and usage in low- and middle-income countries.* London, UK: GSMA.

GSMA & the Cherie Blair Foundation for Women. (2010). *Women & mo-bile: A global opportunity.* London, UK: GSMA.

Hafkin, N. (2002). Gender issues in ICT policy in developing countries: An overview. In *Information and communication technologies and their impact on and use as an instrument for the advance-ment and empowerment of women.* UN-DAW, Seoul, Republic of Korea.

Hofstede, G. (1980). Motivation, leadership, and organization: Do American theories apply abroad? *Organizational Dynamics, 9*(1), 42-63.

Hofstede, G. (1991). *Cultures and organizations: Software of the mind.* London, UK: McGraw-Hill.

Hofstede, G. H., & Hofstede, G. (2001). *Culture's consequences: Comparing values, behaviors, institutions and organizations across nations.* Thousand Oaks, CA: Sage.

Hui, C. H., & Triandis, H. C. (1985). Measurement in cross-cultural psychology: A review and comparison of strategies. *Journal of Cross-Cultural Psychology, 16*(2), 21.

Huyer, S., & Sikoska, T. (2003). *Overcoming the gender digital divide: Understanding ICTs and their potential for the empowerment of women.* INSTRAW.

INTEL. (2012). Women and the web: Bridging the Internet gap and creating new global opportunities in low and middle-income countries. Retrieved from http://www.intel.com/content/www/us/en/technology-in-education/women-in-the-web.html

International Telecommunications Union (ITU). (2011). *ICT facts and figures.* Geneva, Switzerland: ITU.

International Telecommunications Union (ITU). (2012a). *ICT facts and figures.* Geneva, Switzerland: ITU.

International Telecommunications Union (ITU). (2012b). *Measuring the information society.* Geneva, Switzerland: ITU.

International Telecommunications Union (ITU). (2013). *Measuring the information society.* Geneva, Switzerland: ITU.

International Telecommunications Union (ITU). (2014). *Manual for measuring ICT access and use by households and individuals.* Geneva, Switzerland: ITU.

ITU-UNESCO. (2013). *Doubling digital opportunities.* Geneva, Switzerland: Broadband Commission Working Group.

Lichtenstein, S., & Williamson, K. (2006). Understanding consumer adoption of internet banking: An interpretive study in the Australian banking context. *Journal of Electronic Commerce Research, 7*(2),

50-66.

Manobi Development Foundation. (n.d.). Empowering women. Retrieved on September 18, 2014 from http://www.manobi.sn/sites/founda-tion/website/?M=2&SM=3

Marchewka, J., Liu, C., & Kostiwa, K. (2007). An application of the UTAUT model for understanding student perceptions using course management software. *Communications of the IIMA, 7*(2), 93-104.

Meggiolaro, L., Pallas, S., Davies, T. G., & Treakle, J. (2013). *Connecting people, sharing knowledge, increasing transparency: Using the land portal to increase access to open data, share best practices and monitor women's land rights.* Proceedings from the Annual World Bank Conference on Land and Poverty, Washington, DC: World Bank.

Nabi, R. L., Southwell, B., & Hornik, R. (2002). Predicting intentions versus predicting behaviors: Domestic violence prevention from a theory of reasoned action perspective. *Health Communication, 14*(4), 429-449.

Oleksy, W., Just, E., & Zapedowska-Kling, K. (2012). Gender issues in in-formation and communication technologies (ICTs). *Journal of In-formation, Communication and Ethics in Society, 10*(2), 107-120.

Prasad, K. (2012). *Mobile communication for sustainable development: Change and challenges in South Asia.* Paper presented at the Pro-ceedings of M4D 2012 28-29, New Delhi, India.

Qualcomm. (2014). Transforming women's livelihoods through mobile broadband. Retrieved from https://www.qualcomm.com/docu-ments/transforming-womens-livelihoods-through-mobile-broad-band

Rogers, E. (1995). *Diffusion of innovations.* New York, NY: Free Press.

Ruth, S. (2012). Is there a digital divide? Check the numbers. *IEEE, 16*(4), 4.

Schwartz, S. H. (1999). A theory of cultural values and some implications for work. *Applied Psychology: An International Review, 48*, 23-

47.

Schwartz, S. J., Montgomery, M., & Briones, E. (2006). The role of identity in acculturation among immigrant people: Theoretical propositions, empirical questions, and applied recommendations. *Human Development, 49*, 1-30.

Schwartz, S. J., Zamboanga, B., Meca, A., & Ritchie, R. (2013). Identity around the world. New Directions for Child and *Adolescent Development, 138*, 1-18.

Sharma, M., & Kanekar, A. (2007). Theory of reasoned action & theory of planned behavior in alcohol and drug education. *Journal of Alcohol and Drug Education, 51*(1), 3.

Stavrositu, C., & Sundar, S. S. (2012). Does blogging empower women? Exploring the role of agency and community. *Journal of Computer Mediated Communication, 17*(4), 369-386.

Tajfel, H., & Turner, J. C. (1986). *The social identity theory of intergroup behavior.* In S. Worchel & W. G. Austin (Eds.). *The psychology of intergroup relations* (pp. 7-24). Chicago, IL: Nelson-Hall.

Thrasher, R. G., Andrew, D.P.S., & Mahony, D. F. (2011). The efficacy of a modified theory of reasoned action to explain gambling behavior in college students. *Journal of Gambling Studies, 27*(3), 499-516.

UNICEF. (2002). Birth registration—Right from the start. *Innocenti Digest, 9*, 34.

UNICEF. (2014). In the United Republic of Tanzania, a new solution for birth registration. Retrieved on September 9, 2014 from http://www.unicef.org/infobycountry/tanzania_71827.html

Van Slyke, C., Lou, H., & Day, J. (2002). The impact of perceived innovation characteristics on intention to use groupware. *Information Resources Management Journal, 15*(1), 1-12.

Venkatesh, V., & Morris, M. G. (2000). Why don't men ever stop to ask for directions? Gender, social influence, and their role in technology acceptance and usage behavior. *MIS Quarterly, 24*(1), 115-139.

Venkatesh, V., Morris, M., Davis, G., & Davis, F. (2003). User acceptance of information technology: Toward a unified view. *MIS Quarterly,* *27*(3), 425-478.

Wong, K.-T., Teo, T., & Russo, S. (2012). Influence of gender and computer teaching efficacy on computer acceptance among Malaysian student teachers: An extended technology acceptance model. *Australasian Journal of Educational Technology, 28*(7), 1190-1207.

Zhou, G., & Xu, J. (2007). Adoption of educational technology: How does gender matter? *International Journal of Teaching and Learning in Higher Education, 19*(2), 140-153

About the Author

Dr. Deirdre E. Bradley currently runs her own consulting company, creating or transforming courseware with the latest advancements in technology and psychology to produce courses that engage, educate, and empower adult learners.

Dr. Bradley has designed, created, and led the learning and development departments for several Silicon Valley start-ups. She has been an invited speaker for numerous organizations, including the United Nations (UNCCC), USAID, the National Association of Historically Black Colleges and Universities, and the American Psychological Association. Her current research focuses on psychological factors affecting women's adoption of mobile technology, and the effective design of mobile apps for women with little to no literacy skills.

Dr. Bradley's professional career has been a combination of research and teaching, with a focus on international development. As a researcher for NASA, Dr. Bradley worked to develop an early warning famine system using satellite data. While attending graduate school at U.C. Davis, she conducted research on crop stress physiology, earning an M.Sc. in plant physiology and completing the course requirements for a PhD in agricultural (international development) economics. Shifting her career from research to education, Dr. Bradley worked with the USDA Office of International Cooperation and Development to design and administer international training programs for sponsors including the World Bank, the

UN Food and Agricultural Agency, and the US Agency for International Development. She later served as the Associate Director for USAID's Global Agricultural Training Program, working with over 62 developing countries. Dr. Bradley has lived and worked in Peru and Taiwan.

MARGINALIZATION AND THE SEARCH FOR
IDENTITY AND AUTHENTICITY IN VIRTUAL SPACES:
A QUALITATIVE STUDY

Jon Cabiria, PhD, Fielding Graduate University, USA

Abstract: For some lesbian and gay people, the imposition of a heteronormative social model requires the repression of one's true identity and
living an inauthentic life. Researchers have indicated that this can lead to
damaging psychological and sociological effects. In fact for some the dissonance between one's inner sense of self and the outer presentation of self
can lead to the development of loneliness, isolation, depression, low self-
esteem, and withdrawal. The phenomenon to be addressed by this research
project was to understand how some marginalized lesbian and gay people
perceived their engagement in online social activities and its relevance in
their real-world lives.

In this grounded-theory qualitative study, the experiences of social
interactions were analyzed through the theoretical lenses of lesbian and
gay lifespan development theories, as well as Fredrickson's broaden-and-
build theory of positive emotions. Conceptual approaches included explorations into authenticity, belongingness, psychological well-being, support
systems, and self-esteem. The research questions that guided the design
and the discussion of the results sought to understand the experiences of
selected lesbian and gay participants in their online social activities, and
to discover whether positive benefits experienced online were applicable
to real-world lives. Ultimately, the goal was to discover whether online
social activities could be recommended as therapeutic tools for some marginalized people.

Research results indicated that the participants experienced a sense of
belongingness, support, improved well-being, higher self-esteem, authenticity, and optimism when engaging in online social activities. Furthermore, some participants indicated that the experiences in their virtual lives
prompted them to carry over the positive benefits into their real-world

lives. Based on this, there appears to be support for the broaden-and-build theory of positive emotion, the permeability between real and virtual lives, and the therapeutic usefulness of online social sites.

Keywords: authenticity, belonging, broaden-and-build, gay, grounded theory, lesbian, lifespan development, marginalization, permeability, positive psychology, qualitative, second life, social support, stigma, virtual worlds

Introduction
The self is not something that one finds.
It is something that one creates.
– Thomas Szasz, 1973

The "place" of the lesbian woman and the gay man in the United States has been much debated over the past 50+ years. While the U.S. is often touted, even self-described, as the "land of the free" and a place of equal opportunity, it doesn't take long to discover that these are, on occasion, ideals to aspire to rather than actual realities. For lesbian and gay people, the struggle for equality at times mirrors those of other historically maligned groups in U.S. history, while they also experience divergent struggles unique only to them. Freedom and opportunity, at least as an openly lesbian or gay person, has often been, and can still be, elusive (Raushenbush, 2014). Fortunately, the advent of the age of the Internet, and subsequent technological evolutions that brought to the world online social networks, not only revolutionized how people connect and communicate with each other, but also how marginalized individuals and groups use these as tools to overcome outcast status, and to remove the stigma of being "the other."

The study of "the other" has been explored throughout history, with numerous examples of how "the other" presents a real threat to the social order (Marmor, Bieber, & Gold, 1999). While theories abound related to reactions and behaviors toward "the other," society at large still has great difficulty in addressing the harm that is often inflicted upon "the other," often in the name of some personal or group ideology, and arising from something more primal and instinctive (Walker, 1998). Fear of that which is strange or different is a reflexive survival mechanism—survival of the individual and survival of the group. Of course, this is not to say that anything strange or different is dangerous, only that the "other" should be approached with caution until more information has been gathered to provide a more informed opinion. It is at this juncture that prejudice and stigma arise—when more information is not sought, or the information presented is devalued in order to maintain the status quo opinion. This is when "strange" becomes "the other."

Theorists tell us that we need "the other" to set the boundaries of a group norm past which the group might begin to disintegrate (e.g., Coleman, 1990; Durkheim, 1950; Hechter & Opp, 2001; Parsons, 1937; Parsons & Shils, 1951). We look to the other for guidance, against which to compare ourselves, and in that comparison to, we hope, view ourselves more dominantly by subordinating those outside of our sphere of influence. It would appear that the goal of subordinating others who do not follow the socially prescribed norms of a group is another individual and group survival mechanism, as is reaction to that which is strange and different, as described in part by dominance hierarchy theories (see Cummins, 1996; Wilson, 2000). After all, wouldn't the persistence over time of negative attitudes toward "the other" signal some possibility that there is a survival mechanism at play? Conversely, wouldn't the persistence over time of "others" signal the same?

Looking at the role of diversity in society, it would appear that groups need not only social norms to keep the group strong and cohesive, but that groups also need diverse perspectives in order to compete effectively in the larger scheme of social evolution. In essence, it would appear that social groups should be in a constant state of self-reflection and reconstruction.

The concept of social construction is interesting, within this discussion of acceptance or rejection of "the other," in that social construction of "the other" is not the sole result of immutable laws of nature, as theorists who propose an exogenic approach would have us believe (e.g., Locke, Hume, and Mills), but is the result of the variability of social norms, the blending of cultures, and progressive undertakings in light of new insights. All of this could trigger a natural instinct to create social order out of the disruptive influences of change, as proposed in part by endogenic perspectives (e.g., Spinoza, Kant, and Nietzsche). Basically, social construction theories tell us that people, as social beings, instinctively create their social orders based on the environment in which any particular group finds itself (Gergen & Davis, 1985). It would appear that social construction is often born of reactivity rather than proactivity. As the name implies, "social construction" is not an individual process of determining social norms, but a group process that evolves from the collective behaviors and interactions of people who adjust their own individual norms to achieve a social consensus (1985)—arguably a consensus that serves the present but must yield to the future.

A major consideration when discussing the social construction of a group and of that group's relationship to "the other" is how valuable the concept is of one's group and personal identity in the creation of social norms. How a person presents oneself to the world, and how other people perceive that person, constitute one's social identity (Tajfel & Turner, 1986). It would be a logical assumption, then, that group identity would be a representation of the individual identities of that group's membership, aggregated through a process of norming to arrive at the social boundaries ascribed to by the group, and which define the group and its position in the larger social network. This coming together of multiple identities for mutual benefit relates directly to Maslow's Hierarchy of Needs and its description of people's need for a sense of safety and belonging (Maslow, 1968). It is at this juncture—the need to feel safe and the need to belong—that, in a very simplistic manner, "the other" is created who, by virtue of not being a member of the dominant group, is left excluded and vulnerable, neither safe nor wanted.

In 1963, Irving Goffman, a noted sociologist and possibly the most prominent figure in sociology in modern times (Fine & Manning, 2003), discussed social stigma at great length. He indicated that social groups, by virtue of the norms they create for themselves, automatically create labels for those who are outside of their group. Part of this social construction of an outcast includes the building of a set of stereotypical attributes to help identify "the other" and justify the "other's" outcast status. The goal of this process is to either encourage (or force) "the other" to merge with the dominant social system or to become marginalized by it. Most often, the "other" is unable or unwilling to meet the requirements of the dominant group and is segregated from it. Further, in keeping with the need to create clear identities throughout any social system, outcasts are identified as having stigmas. Goffman (1963) noted that stigmas manifest as visible or hidden. Generally, physical characteristics, such as gender, skin color, and some physical conditions may lead to stigmatization of a visible nature and from which the person cannot escape. Other characteristics, such as some mental issues, physical conditions that are internal or not easily viewable, and sexual orientation may be considered hidden stigmas.

While the marginalizing effect of stigmatization is far-ranging and complex, and its relationship to the creation and maintenance of "the other" produces a variety of social change considerations, there is one group of interest that presents a unique glimpse into the effects of hidden stigmas, which can be quite different from those with visible stigmas. Members of sexual minority communities, which include a wide array of sexual orientations and gender identities, represent a matrix of minorities and minorities-within-minorities, and often carry with them multiple stigma labels both visible and hidden. This article will examine the social construction of stigmatized sexual minority individuals and groups, particularly lesbian and gay people, and the quest for safety and belonging. It will be framed within the context of the role of social media as a tool to reduce the negative effects of stigmatization and to increase the sense of safety and belonging—because both are important considerations in the mental and physical health of lesbian and gay individuals—of the social groups to which they belong, and of the strength and continuance of the greater society.

With regard to the role of social media as a tool used to allow "the others" (in this case, gay and lesbian people) a means to find and build community, to construct individual and social identities, and to experience safety and belonging, it is important to note how media has historically been a double-edged sword in many respects. On the one hand, it has been use to promote prejudicial agendas, lending a voice and support to dominant groups at the expense of others. On the other hand, it has also been used as a means to fight this very same prejudicial treatment, allowing the ability of marginalized individuals to form groups, disseminate differing perspectives, and build policy-changing coalitions. From printed materials such as posters, newsletters, newspapers, magazines, and books, to electronic media such as radio, TV, movies, and the Internet, to a wide variety of online social media such as is found in virtual reality, augmented reality, and online social communities and networks, lesbian and gay people have been able to come out of the shadows, gaining incremental but steady acceptance within general society in the United States. In fact, research subsequent to this study found that online social technologies can offer substantial benefits for marginalized people, such as lesbian and gay youth, who experience disproportionate social exclusion and victimization as a result of their sexual orientation (Craig, McInroy, Di Cesare, & Pettaway, 2014). While lesbian and gay people are still not always viewed as accepted members of the dominant society, they can be seen as being in tandem with it on some important touchstones. From "the love that dare not speak its name" as a euphemism for homosexuality (a misinterpretation of Douglas, 1894) to same-sex marriage, media's push and pull role is unquestionable in lesbian and gay people's quest for freedom and equality.

This research review examines how one small group of research study participants used social media to not only find understanding and support from similar others in a virtual space when the real world seemed stigmatizing and dangerous, but how the experience of being able to fully express their identities with similar others, in a community that was accepting and safe, led to surprising real world implications for inclusion. This next section will describe the research methodology, after which the research results will be tied to the practical applications of social inclusion in the digital age.

Research Design

While great achievements have been made in the quest for lesbian and gay freedom and equality in the United States, most recently with the U.S. Supreme Court ruling on June 26, 2015 regarding the case of Obergefell v. Hodges that the 14th Amendment requires all U.S. state laws to recognize same-sex marriages (Supreme Court, 2015), there are still many issues to be addressed. Discrimination, bullying, inadequate health resources, and lack of job security and senior care are just a few social issues requiring ongoing debate and advocacy. Of these, an underlying psychological effect of fear still lingers in many lesbian and gay people, depending upon their life circumstances. We know from research that when marginalized people are able to find and bond with similar others, their physical and mental health demonstrates positive effects. We also know that the advent of the Internet, and of online social networks and communities in particular, has provided ample opportunities for marginalized people to connect with each other and find support. What was not known, until this recent study, was whether the positive benefits of online social engagement had ramifications for real-world benefits. Essentially, what was the experience of marginalized lesbian and gay people in the real world once they had utilized virtual worlds to seek a positive sense of self in the real world?

Concepts

The research study focused on many concepts related to the existence of marginalized lesbian and gay people. Five of these concepts will be the focus of this research study review: authenticity; belongingness; psychological well-being; support systems; and self-esteem.

Authenticity refers to a person's ability to live a life that is open, honest, and a representative outward expression of one's inner sense of self. For many people, who perceive themselves as having stigmas that can be hidden, such as those experienced by some lesbian and gay people, living an authentic life becomes a constant negotiation around how to behave, what to say, whom to trust, and what facades to use. Living "in the closet," a term to describe suppression of one's lesbian or gay identity in favor of a more heteronormative façade, can take a psychological and physical toll over time, and can be especially destructive for lesbian and gay teens during their adolescent, identity-formative years. This can have significant effects on a person's ability to maintain solid relationships, and can have negative repercussions that last a lifetime (Meyer, 2003). This research study was designed to better understand the role of online social engagement in the expression of one's authentic self.

Belonginess, as one of Maslow's Hierarchy of Needs, is a key component related to the instinctive drive in human beings to relate with one another. Humans desire to be part of a group, and to identify with a group, in order to feel safe while at the same time being in a better position to achieve their own goals through the support of that group. For lesbian and gay people, a sense of isolation can often be the byproduct of being open about one's sexual orientation, leading to ostracization or being "in the closet" and using energy to keep distant from others for fear of being found out. Recent research related to how and when sexual minority people "come out" found that online friends are a critical component in the support needed for successful adaptation of a lesbian or gay identity in a heteronormative society. This current research study was designed as a means to better understand the role of online social sites in the creation of a personal sense of belonging, and how that belonging produced positive benefits for the marginalized person.

Psychological well-being is a powerful concept, and an important consideration when discussing the negative effects of discrimination and marginalization of lesbian and gay people, especially for lesbian and gay youth. Of concern are the effects of isolation, fear, paranoia, low self-esteem, and possible attempts to self-medicate or self-harm due to the constant stressors that can come with living in an environment that is perceived as hostile and even life threatening. While there have been great gains in social acceptance of lesbian and gay people, there are still large areas of the country, pockets of urban and rural areas, and even individual family units that remain intolerant, even violently intolerant. In contrast, online social communities and networks can provide lesbian and gay people with significantly safer spaces in which to congregate and to receive valuable support services (Craig, McInroy, Di Cesare, & Pettaway, 2014). This research project explored the meaning of living in a real-world environment perceived as dangerous, and how an online social environment might have mitigated the psychological harm experienced in the real world.

Support systems are a key aspect of life within any social community. There are numerous theories that account for how and why a strong social system works, such as social capital theory (e.g., Coleman, 1988), which essentially tells us that we help others in order to be helped by others, Triver's theory of reciprocal altruism (1971), which explores how we provide for each other based on reciprocity, Hamilton's genetic basis for social support motivations (1964), and Batson's empathy-altruism theory (1981), which informs us that people are motivated by genuine concern for the welfare of others. When support systems are perceived as lacking, as can be the case with marginalized people, there are significant ramifications for a variety of considerations, such as physical and mental healthcare, employment, information, and a sense of well-being. Lesbian and gay people, more than heterosexual people, are more likely to have online friends, and to feel that these online relationships can be more valuable and significant when it comes to providing social support (Belous, Wampler, & Warmels-Herring, 2015) This research study examines the role of online social engagement in the attainment of social support, and the meaning that this support gives to the lives of marginalized lesbian and gay people.

Self-esteem describes how a person evaluates and values oneself. It often reflects how someone perceives her or his worth to others, and how one's level of self-esteem can have a strong influence on one's psychological state of mind. Given that most people are inherently social and require approval from others in some fashion, a lack of approval (or a sense of devaluation by others) can result in significantly decreased self-esteem, leading to mental health issues including depression, suicidal thoughts or actions, risky behaviors, and strained relationships. For the marginalized lesbian or gay person, negative social messages, whether from within the family, from religious organizations, or through various media messages, can aggregate over time to create a profile of the lesbian or gay person as not good enough, damaged, dangerous, unholy, and perverse (Pachankis, 2006; Pachankis & Goldfried, 2006). This research study attempted to raise the possible benefits of a supportive online social environment and the meaning it produced related to one's self-perceptions of value.

Research Questions

Given that online social networks and communities are recent phenomena, even when considering the rapidity of technological growth over the past few decades, there is relatively little research on the topic of the benefit of online social engagement for marginalized people in general and lesbian and gay people specifically. Furthermore, the venue for this study, Second Life, was at the time a significant evolution in online social media, in that it offered greater sensory experiences, such as visuals and audio, than existing popular social media, and gave users control over the creation of their avatar identities and the environment in which these avatars operated. For this, too, there was little in the way of social sciences research. The paucity of existing research indicated that a qualitative study would be an appropriate initial step, and that grounded theory would help generate potential hypotheses for future quantitative studies.

The research question that guided this research was as follows: What are the experiences of selected lesbian and gay participants in their Second Life activities?

Secondary questions sought to discover whether any gains experienced in the virtual world were transferable to the real world, and whether the use of virtual worlds could be recommended as a therapeutic tool for some marginalized gay and lesbian people.

Theoretical Framework

Several theories were used to frame this research project. It has been noted that marginalization can have significant effects on lifespan development, especially if experienced during the critical identity-formative years of adolescence (Nickolas, 1995). It has also been proposed in some human development theories that some lesbian and gay people experience lifespan development differently than other people. It made sense, therefore, that theories related to lesbian and gay lifespan development would be a significant part of the framework for how online social interactions might facilitate the progression of lesbian and gay identity development in a way that real-world interactions might obstruct. The main considerations were that most lesbian and gay people are brought up in a heteronormative environment, are usually perceived as and treated as heterosexual, and are expected to adopt a heterosexual identity (Perez, DeBord, & Bieschke, 2000). The suppression of one's inherent sexual orientation, a key facet of one's identity, can create a deep-rooted sense of inauthenticity, possibly leading to any number of mental health, physical health, and social relationship disorders. Several developmental theories explain this phenomenon, and can be utilized to set the foundation for what draws lesbian and gay people to online social interactions as an escape from a repressive real-world environment. Additionally, these developmental theories can assist in explaining developmental metamorphoses as a result of online social interactions with similar others. Theories such as the four-stage Troiden model (Troiden, 1989, 1988, 1984/1985, 1970; Troiden & Goode, 1980), Cass's six-stage model (1979), Coleman's two-stage Coming Out model (1982), and the five-stage Scrivner model (Scrivner, 1984) encompass the major theories in lesbian and gay development. All four of these models strive to explain how lesbian and gay development diverges from heterosexual development. It is important to note, at this point, that the majority of research related to these models has been focused on gay men, although the Cass model sought to level the research field by being more diverse in its explorations. The essence of these models can be reduced to the possibility that "being in the closet" or being ostracized by "coming out of the closet" can produce an identity moratorium of indeterminate length until a path for an authentic identity can be achieved.

Another key theory was also used to help frame this study and explain the research results. Research into positive emotions over the past two decades has yielded some interesting findings related to coping and resiliency skills. Of note is Fredrickson's broaden-and-build theory of positive emotions (1998, 2001) which proposes that positive emotions help people to deal with difficult situations, and explains how people with positive emotions tend to benefit from them during times of stress and uncertainty (Tugade & Fredrickson, 2004). It is theorized that engagement in online social venues by lesbian and gay people can lead to positive emotions, as described by Fredrickson, leading to a broadening of perspectives beyond the focus on problems such as stigmatization and marginalization to help the individual discover meaningfulness and authenticity.

Participants

Participants for this study were drawn from a variety of online social groups that catered to professional people such as educators. The rationale was that online professional groups would tend to be frequented by credible members who would also have a scholarly interest in this type of study. Other sources included lesbian and gay online social groups that had a stable and active long-term membership focused on support and advocacy. Potential participants were solicited through postings in these members-only forums, vetted through a series of questionnaires, and selected based on criteria related to the extent of their online social activities, their age (over 18), and their lesbian or gay self-identification. Additionally, inclusion factors required the ability to speak and write English well enough to comprehend the study materials and the process, and their availability to meet in the Second Life virtual world. For consistency, it was also required that all participants utilized Second Life as their main online social outlet.

Of 4,500–5,000 people contacted to be a part of the study, approximately 130 filled out the initial online demographic questionnaire. Of that group, approximately 30 met the requirements for inclusion in the study and were invited to participate, and 17 accepted the invitation. Fourteen applicants followed through, with 11 completing the whole study.

Data were collected in several different ways. Once the initial demographic and inclusion questionnaire was submitted, accepted participants completed two other questionnaires: a "Real Life" questionnaire and a "Second Life" questionnaire. Each questionnaire asked similar questions about psychological and sociological phenomena in the participant's real world and virtual world lives. In total, 129 questions were asked, split almost evenly between the two documents. The researcher then set up a series of one-hour interviews in a private virtual space set up in Second Life. The conversations, based on semi-structured interviews, followed up on the responses found in the two questionnaires. The conversations were text-based and were saved for analysis. Subsequent interviews were conducted with the participants to clarify points of interest or to seek further information. Additionally, the researcher reviewed notes and insights with the participants to check for accuracy of interpretation. After the data were collected and analyzed, participants were contacted and presented with the write-up of their individual interviews to once again check for interpretation and accuracy. Upon approval from the participants, the data results were formally written up. Every step of the process was guided by best practices in the protection of the identity and well-being of the participants, and in accordance with APA ethical guidelines for research and the institutional review board at Fielding Graduate University. Names used in the research results are pseudonyms.

Findings and Applications

Using a process of software coding to identify basic concepts, hand coding was then used to develop a more organic approach to the content in order to draw out the nuance of the participants' narratives. This comprehensive questionnaire and interview process yielded quite a few interesting results—in fact, much more than can be adequately addressed in this summary article. This discussion will focus solely on the five main points of interest indicated in the introduction to this study, namely authenticity, belongingness, psychological well-being, support systems, and self-esteem.

Authenticity

Authenticity can be defined as people's ability to present themselves to others in an honest, representative manner that represents who they believe themselves to be, even in the face of social forces that might try to force identity repression in order to meet existing social norms for identity expression. From an existentialist perspective, one can look to Heidegger, Kierkegaard, Nietzsche, and Sartre for insights into one's inner truth exposed, regardless of social construction pressures, or to Fromm, who indicated that authenticity was a conscious exploration of the benefits of social construction by the individual who ascribed to social norms as part of their identity presentation. In the end, it comes down to one's subjective truth and the ability to live it in an open and honest manner.

Danielle was a 59-year-old lesbian from the Northwest United States, which is also how she presented herself in Second Life. She spent about 50 hours a month in Second Life, mostly as a social adjunct to her real-life social activities. She clearly wanted to present herself in an authentic manner in real life and in her virtual life. She appeared to want to reject labels, and found Second Life to be a great place to just be "a person" rather than "a lesbian person."

> I don't think of myself like a lesbian lady all of the time. I am just a lady who happens to like other ladies, but I am so much more than that. I wasn't sure I was even going to do this project with you because I was worried that it would make me focus on just being homosexual, which would totally negate all the other things about me.

Clearly, Danielle had reflected deeply on her identity and was careful to manage it so that she presented herself in a multifaceted manner, regardless of her online or offline persona.

In contrast to Danielle, Henry, a 55-year-old gay male from the mid-Atlantic region of the United States, and also a frequent user of Second Life, told a different story. For Henry, his adolescent developmental years were filled with fear and self-loathing as he tried to reject and hide his homosexuality. For him, having an authentic and honest relationship was difficult. His life was filled with dissonance as he tried to manage multiple identities as a heterosexual with family and work, and a gay man with select close friends. As he grew older, the stress of this duplicity began to wear him down. When he discovered Second Life, it made him more aware of this dissonance, but also prompted deeper reflection on who he was and how he wanted to present himself to the world. It was a search for personal authenticity.

> I know how pathetic it sounds but I don't care. I feel like I am part of something when I am with my friends in Second Life. When I am not in Second Life, I don't really feel a part of anything. . . . This has me thinking that maybe Second Life is a wonderful learning experience for me. I am learning how to be myself again. Maybe the happy me that is in this fake world [Second Life] will come out in me in my real world. I want to look into that more.

Jennie, a 40-year-old lesbian living in Northern California, was a successful businesswoman who felt constrained by her sexual orientation. On the one hand, she enjoyed the power and self-efficacy of her corporate position and all of the benefits it entailed, but she was also concerned about the personal cost as a result of working in a climate that had homophobic undertones. Similarly to Henry, the duplicity of her life was a constant source of anxiety. Even in Second Life she felt uncomfortable being totally open about her full identity, clearly indicating that developmental issues had influenced her ability to form open and authentic relationships.

> I am a really forceful person but the gay thing has me messed up sometimes. I don't know why I am so afraid. . . . I can be freer in Second Life even though it feels uncomfortable to be that open sometimes.

All of the participants indicated issues with authenticity. Most of them struggled with it in real life and found Second Life to be more liberating, but a few had a difficult time breaking old patterns of careful identity management and a life time of suppression, even in a virtual and anonymous environment such as Second Life. For them, authenticity was still an ideal to strive for.

Belongingness

To be in a repressed state in which one's true identity is denied can cause one to suffer:

> . . .systematic harm due to refusal by society of basic rights, denial of a

range of opportunities and social benefits; lack of respect and of social belonging; and forfeiture of the kinds of intimate relationships and love that make personal happiness possible. (Seidman, 2002, p. 30)

Maslow (1968), as well as other sociologists and mental health experts, tells us that the basic drive of social creatures, including human beings, is to find comfort, safety, and well-being when a sense of belongingness is achieved. Infants denied the basics of companionship will suffer from failure to thrive (see Bowlby, 1988; Field, 1988; Harlow, 1958; Spitz, 1945). For marginalized lesbian and gay people, there is a strong desire to find a place—physical and emotional—where they feel as if they belong. For some, this occurred after engaging in online social activities.

Justin was a 55-year-old gay man from the Canadian Northwest. His Second Life avatar appeared to be younger in appearance, and he typically spent about 50 or more hours a month in Second Life. Justin's home was in a rural location and he found it hard to meet other gay people, hence his attraction to Second Life and other online social venues. His few social activities revolved around the lives of his heterosexual friends, which he described as somewhat satisfying, but not fulfilling. He felt more like a "visitor" with his friends. Engagement with online friends, however, produced different results: "My world has opened up. I feel like I belong somewhere. I can be myself."

Thomas, a 36-year-old gay man from a mid-Atlantic state, was open about his sexual orientation to everyone in his real life and in Second Life. However, this openness had not come easily and was marked by many years, during his developmental stages, of fear, self-loathing, and uncertainty. This included an identity moratorium, a common period of time during which no developmental growth occurs while the adolescent or young adult tries to figure out who they are. Community plays a big role in identity development, as Thomas discovered when exploring Second Life.

I am with people who are like me and who have very different life stories but the common one is that we experienced being gay in a lot of similar ways. We talk about this sometimes. . . . We are a community. In some ways, it is more genuine than in real life. There seems to be a lot more empathy for each other's lives, knowing that we are all sort of on the outside of society even though we function in it every day.

Karen, a 24-year-old lesbian from the Pacific Northwest, was raised in a strict religious household. At that point, she had never told anyone in her real life about her sexual orientation. She lived in constant fear of being found out and spent a great deal of energy fabricating a façade in real life, including a series of imaginary boyfriends to help maintain her false front. The inauthenticity, and lack of a sense of belonging, became increasingly stressful. She found relief in Second Life.

> I started to go back on weekends [to a social space in Second Life] and started to see and talk to the same people and we became friends. I became part of this little social club. It was nice. . . . It feels good, I guess. I don't have to feel like I'm lying or trying to fool anybody. I can be more like myself.

For Justin, Thomas, and Karen, regardless of their level of openness about their sexual orientation in real life, they found a meaningful, authentic sense of belonging in the virtual social environment. For some, virtual engagements were an important extension of their real-world sense of community and belonging; yet for others, it was the only place where they could feel open, comfortable, safe, and wanted. Even identity moratorium, the obstacle to finding oneself and one's place in the world, was lifted, allowing the developmental process to resume. The power of feeling "belonged" cannot be underestimated.

Psychological Well-being

It is clear that people require strong and meaningful social interactions in order to feel healthy and to be healthy. Research has shown that the ability to live openly according to one's sexual orientation and to be a part of a group of similar others produces a sense of well-being and contentment. Furthermore, sexual identity development, along with perceptions of social support, plays a major role in the well-being of lesbian and gay people (Gallor & Fassinger, 2010; Meyer, 2003). Conversely, significant relationships have been noted between increased levels of minority stress and mental health problems, including suicidal ideation, depression, and

anxiety (Kuyper & Fokkema, 2011; Meyer, 1995). Many of the health issues and stresses appear to be related to lesbian and gay people who adopt
a heterosexual identity rather than deal with a social environment perceived as hostile or even dangerous. During an extended period of sexual
orientation repression, health issues surface and tend to become extreme
over time (Kuyper & Fokkema, 2011). For Justin, the virtual world of Second Life became a place to practice coming out and to learn how to live
as a gay man in public while experiencing the healthful benefits that come
with living more authentically.

> I think I am learning to relate to people better because Second Life
> is like practice for me in a safer environment. It's not so damaging if
> I make social mistakes in Second Life. I can learn from the mistakes
> and maybe that will also help me in real life. I don't know. I think it
> can. . . . For me, Second Life has been a way out of a rather depress-
> ing isolation, and I have been noticing the changes in my mental state
> (increased self-confidence, and a mood of enthusiasm, and positive
> anticipation) as my Second Life has been unfolding.

Rory is a 25-year-old Caucasian gay male from Brooklyn, New York.
He is completely in the closet. In Second Life, he presents as a 25-year-old
Caucasian gay male and spends about 60 hours a month in Second Life,
where he is out to everyone. Similar to Justin, Rory also expressed a sense
of well-being as a result of his Second Life experiences.

> I feel like a big weight is lifted off my shoulders when I am in Second
> Life because I don't always have to be watching what I say or do. I
> don't have to worry about slipping up. When I go to bed after a night
> in Second Life, I sleep really good and feel better the next day.

Albert is a 30-year-old Caucasian gay male currently living in Eng-
land, though who was born and raised in the U.S. Regarding his level of
being out, most of his friends and some of his immediate family know
that he is gay. He has remained closeted to neighbors and coworkers. In
Second Life, Albert is also a 30-year-old Caucasian gay male and he is
completely out. He spends more than 30 hours a month in Second Life.
Albert's story is aligned with Rory's, in that both are closeted to some ex-

tent in the real world, yet completely open about their sexual orientation in the virtual world. Also, like Rory and Justin, Albert felt a strong sense of well-being when participating in online social engagements.

> I am more comfortable being gay in Second Life, maybe because I know that no one can hurt me or look badly at me. I also know that I can just teleport away if someone is an ass but that has never happened. I really feel freer there.

Billy is a 61-year-old Caucasian gay male from Chicago. He is a practicing Muslim and he is not out about his sexual orientation to anyone in real life. In Second Life, Billy explores different identities, genders, and ages. He is out to everyone in Second Life, keeps his main sexual identity as a gay male, and spends about 40 hours a month in Second Life.

> I cannot be out because I fear for my safety. The Muslim community is not tolerant of homosexuality. I am a loner all day. When I go to Second Life, I can be free and I talk with other people who are like me.

Justin, later on the interview process, noted his experiences when socializing in Second Life that seemed to sum up the general experiences of all of the participants.

> I noticed a month or so after entering the Second Life gay community that my attitude, bearing, general sense of well-being had taken a significant boost. . . . I noticed that I'd gone from a feeling of chronic exhaustion to a sense of almost euphoric energy and started to connect that feeling to my time in Second Life.

Support Systems

Social support is often associated with an increase sense of feeling safe. People who lack social support in the real world can discover that virtual social communities might be important factors in supporting their well-being. Those who reported challenges when in real-world social situations and relationships as a result of their repressed sexual orientation have identified the Internet as a valuable resource for support (McKenna & Bargh, 2000). In fact, an online connection to similar others may be crucial for lesbian and gay people because they are more likely to experience stigma and social marginalization in the real world (GLSENC, 2013; Hillier, Mitchell, & Ybarra, 2012; Mustanski, Lyons, & Garcia, 2011). As found in this study, and supported by subsequent research, lesbian and gay people view online spaces as safe places to receive support from friends (GLSENC, 2013; Hillier, Horsely, & Kurdas, 2004); they say that these online social communities can be safer and more supportive for them to socialize in than real-world social communities (Hillier & Harrison, 2007). Rory, Justin, and Henry discovered how they became comfortable in their virtual social environments, and how, when expressing their concerns with their new online friends over the duplicitous nature of their real-world lives, they discovered that they were not alone in this. They had found similar others with whom they could relate in a way that was often more meaningful than their real-world social engagements.

> Rory: I look forward to meeting my friends there because we have so much fun and we can be so open. I like my real friends too, but these friends I can trust and count on because they will not leave me. My friends in my neighborhood might leave me if they knew [that I was gay], so that is a big difference. . . . I go on Second Life so that I can just be myself.

> Justin: I find that I've built a set of friends here . . . virtual friends, but still friends. I see many of them on a daily or near daily basis. I find my friends in Second Life fill that need . . . the need for a group in which I feel completely at ease.

> Henry: It brought new life to my life. . . . I have friends again. I go dancing. There are things that interest me and that I look forward to. . . . There are familiar places, people that I know, things to do. I feel like I am a part of something. In some ways, I am a part of something in Second Life more than I am a part of anything in real life. . . . It feels good to know that I am not so alone in the world anymore.

Self-esteem

Many of the participants' responses to the questionnaire related to their real-world experiences indicated a sense of loneliness, isolation, and depression as a result of either being closeted or unable to fully relate to their real-world family, friends, and co-workers. Additionally, due to the negative attitudes of society toward lesbian and gay people, many of the participants indicated a sense of low self-esteem. Similarly to a sense of increased well-being as a result of their virtual world social engagements, it would make sense that the participants would also express a sense of higher self-esteem.

Freda was a 42-year-old Caucasian lesbian from a north central state. She is out to everyone. In Second Life, she is also a 42-year-old Caucasian lesbian female, is out to everyone, and spends varying amounts of time each month in Second Life. During her adolescent developmental years, she increasingly doubted her own value, as constant social and media information told her that being a lesbian was a deficiency, a perversion, and evil in the eyes of God.

> I thought I was going to hell for years. . . . Nothing like suddenly finding yourself, then realizing that "God and society" hated you. . . . I, at that point, knew it was a bad thing. Only later did I figure it out and I am okay. . . . It is hard not to dislike yourself to some degree when you believe everyone else dislikes you because of this one thing. . . . I think I would have been happier sooner. I would not have felt alone, isolated, and confused.

Karen picked up on this all-too-familiar feeling and compared it to her virtual world sense of self: "I like how I act in Second Life and I wouldn't change it. I feel really more like myself even if it feels strange to be myself because I'm not used to it."

Vito was a 33-year-old Caucasian gay male from Utah, a non-practicing Mormon, and completely in the closet. In Second Life, he presents as an 18-year-old Caucasian gay male and spends about 50 hours a month in Second Life, where he is out to everyone. He approaches his virtual world activities with a sense of hope and optimism. As he becomes stronger in Second Life, he thinks of how to become stronger in real life. It is clear that the negativity he felt about himself was dissipating as a result of the authenticity, sense of belongingness, and support that he was experiencing in the virtual social environment.

When good things happen in Second Life, I am bound to learn how to make those same good things happen in real life. And I know that I will get stronger about being an out gay person in real life because I am really enjoying being an out gay person in Second Life, and it is getting harder to go back in the closet every time I leave Second Life. Changes are a comin'!

While it is not the purpose of a qualitative study to generalize findings beyond the participants involved in the study, it is clear that the preponderance of similarities in experiences among this study's participants, supported by subsequent studies, can inform us that there is a level of comfort in saying that there are a great many benefits that arise when some lesbian and gay people with repressed sexual orientation identities in the real world engage in online social interactions. Among these are the discovery and expression of an authentic self, feeling a sense of belonging among a group of similar others, development of a sense of well-being and contentment, recognition and appreciation of the value of support systems as part of the ongoing identity development process, and increased self-esteem as negativity related to past cultural influences is replaced by positivity and hope for a better future.

Connection to Positive Psychology

These few narratives demonstrate how lesbian and gay identity construction is often obstructed in real life due to social pressures to adopt heteronormative identities. It is evident from this study that, in Second Life, this repression can be surfaced, explored, and replaced by openness that allows for resumption of a more authentic identity. Throughout the narratives, expressions of relief, a sense of belonging, and feelings of authenticity, among others, indicated positive effects that encouraged the participants to continue to seek out ways to maintain and increase the positive effects that they experienced in Second Life in their real lives. This opens up a discussion related to the theoretical underpinning of this research project—Fredrickson's broaden-and-build theory of positive emotions.

As noted earlier, this theory proposes that resilience and coping within stressful and negative environments can be brought about through small positive experiences. Fredrickson (2001) hypothesized that when people are exposed to negative experiences, they tend to redirect their focus onto the problem. This prevents them from accessing the wealth of cognitive associations that lie outside of that narrow focus, essentially reducing their ability to creatively solve the problem or to see it in a different light. However, Fredrickson also noted that when people are exposed to positive emotions, they tend to make better use of their cognitive associations, are more able to engage in discovery and creativity, and tend to be able to apply more creative, positive solutions to their problems or situations. In this way, when exposed to a meaningful positive stimulus, the person can react in a manner that causes her or him to explore potential solutions that may lie outside of the problem itself. Once a solution has been achieved, the benefit of that solution engenders further solution-creating capabilities to be applied to other negative effects and situations (Fredrickson, 2001).

In this study, the evidence to support this theory is quite compelling. Repeatedly, participants note how the positive experiences they gained in Second Life carry over into their real lives. Some mention how they have gained hope for a better real life; others note how they found a lost part of themselves and now plan to incorporate that desirable lost part into their real lives. For some, the effects are dynamic; for others, the effects are only just now starting to be realized. Given the relatively brief duration of this study, it was not possible to predict how lasting these benefits would be, but it appeared, at least for some participants, that real-life changes were happening.

Real World and Virtual World Permeability

A running theme throughout many of the participants' narratives was this sense of increasing connection between the real world and the virtual world. For some participants, authenticity was often noted as a benefit when exploring identity development in the virtual environment, and how that authenticity was making its way into the participants' real-world lives. Other participants indicated a juxtaposition in real and virtual world experiences, with the virtual experiences being more "real" due to the ability to be more open and honest, and the real world being more "inauthentic" due to the need to repress one's true nature. Over time, the reality of the virtual world appeared to be making its way into the real-world lives of the participants. This permeability between real and virtual worlds suggests interesting psychological and sociological uses for virtual social communities and networks.

Implications for Psychologists

As indicated throughout many of the participants' experiences, in the real world lesbian and gay people face a multitude of challenges related to their sexual orientations, even in this climate of increasing tolerance. For some, the pressures of the local social system keep them repressed, while for others there is little real-world access to lesbian and gay communities. Certainly therapists who work with such populations have a variety of suggestions and treatments that they can provide their clients to help ease them into a supportive environment. For some clients, online social communities and networks may be a useful approach to the goal of living a more fulfilling and authentic life. Some of the narratives that emerged from this study showed how the participants evolved in their thinking that sexual orientation was a behavior to, instead, view sexual orientation as a valuable part of an identity. For the therapist, familiarity with online social sites could be an important addition to a comprehensive services offering, especially related to issues of sexual orientation identity.

Limitations

There are a few important considerations related to the design of this study. While generalizability is not a stated goal in qualitative research, it is still important to note the limiting conditions of this study. First, lesbian women and gay men might experience lifespan development differently and, therefore, the positive experiences of their online social activities, especially related to identity development, could well follow different paths. Similarly, the age range of the participants was broad, as were their race, culture, and socioeconomic status (SES), which would thus have an influence on their perceptions and experiences within the online social environment. Of course, the results can only reflect perceptions and experiences relevant to Second Life, and only by these participants, and cannot be construed to be applicable to lesbian and gay people, or other marginalized people, utilizing other online social venues.

Future Research

Research into the effects on marginalized people and their use of online social communities and networks is in its infancy. A starting point would be to further explore the limitations noted above with regard to age, gender, race, culture, SES, and type of online social venues. As future researchers build upon this information, the collective body of research will, at some point, be able to claim findings that are generalizable to larger populations, as well as provide insights into the uniqueness of each individual experience. Certainly there are many avenues to explore related to social experiences, far beyond virtual worlds. Augmented reality (which overlays digital imagery onto real-world environments), artificial intelligence and robots (used for companionship and other human-machine interactions), and fully immersive virtual environments produced by head-mounted displays (e.g., Oculus Rift). Virtual reality products such as High Fidelity and Sansar will focus on the social interaction aspects of Oculus Rift by creating persistent, user-created, and highly interactive virtual worlds—essentially the next generation of Second Life.

Regardless of the digital format, future research will be needed to explore how these products and experiences affect brain function, the senses, social and emotional development, and expression of identity, to name a few areas of inquiry. For marginalized groups, even as social intelligence evolves, there will always be marginalizing social influences that research into digital social opportunities can help us to better understand and to address.

Conclusion

Referring back to the goals of this study and the research questions that directed its design and implementation, the primary experiences of the lesbian and gay participants who engaged in social activities via digital mediation had several common elements, most notably the desire to live more authentic lives in the real world as a result of their virtual world activities. The achievement of authenticity appears to have had as a prerequisite finding similar others with whom to develop a sense of belonging, and from whom to receive support. This led to a greater sense of well-being and increased self-esteem, allowing for the willingness to live more openly, honestly, and authentically. The research indicated that the experience of authenticity in the virtual world highlighted the dissonance between the participants' inner and outer lives, creating discontent. This led to the desire to live authentically in their real-world lives. The findings in this study indicated the potential for virtual social activities as therapeutic tools for marginalized people, possibly initiated by a knowledgeable therapist.

In the end, this is a study about positive media effects. All too often, digital media research and anecdotal popular discourse focus on the negative effects produced by our digital lives. We hear about Internet addiction, online disinhibition leading to sociopathic and psychopathic behaviors, the decline of social skills, an increase in narcissism, reduced attention span, increased aggression as a result of violent content in digital games . . . the list goes on. Yet in many ways it would be correct to note how our digital activities have presented us with innumerable positive effects as well. For the participants in this study, engagement in virtual worlds began to change their real worlds in meaningful, substantive ways. They learned how to be true to themselves and to others. This authenticity required a safe, welcoming place that offered support and a sense of belonging, where identity and self-esteem issues could be explored and developed. Sometimes the real world cannot provide, or easily provide, what is needed to effect social change. Sometimes the virtual world has the information and support a person needs to survive and thrive . . . not only to experience the positive aspects of an online social community or network, but also to be able to take advantage of the permeability of virtuality and bring those benefits into the real world.

References

Batson, C. D. (1987). Prosocial motivation: is it ever truly altruistic? In L. Berkowitz (Ed.), *Advances in Experimental Social Psychology*, pp. 65-122. New York: Academic Press.

Batson, C. D., Duncan, B. D., Ackerman, P., Buckley, T., & Birch, K. (1981). Is empathic emotion a source of altruistic motivation? *Journal of Personality and Social Psychology,40*(2),290-302.

Bowlby, J. (1988). *Attachment, communication, and the therapeutic process. A secure base: Parent-child attachment and healthy human development.* New York, Basic Books.

Cass, V. C. (1979, Spring). Cass model of gay & lesbian identity formation (adapted from Homosexual identity formation: A theoretical model). *Journal of Homosexuality, 4*(3), 220.

Coleman, E. (1982). Developmental stages of the coming-out process. In J. Gonsiorek (Ed.), *Homosexuality and psychotherapy: A practitioner's handbook of affirmative models*. New York: Haworth.

Coleman, J. (1988). Social capital in the creation of human capital. *American Journal of Sociology,* Supp. 94, S95-S120.

Coleman, J. (1990). *Foundations of social theory*. Cambridge, MA: Belknap.

Cummins, D. D. (1996). Dominance hierarchies and the evolution of human reasoning. *Minds and Machines, 6*(4), 463-480.

Douglas, A. (1894). Two loves. Reprinted from *The Chameleon*. http://law2.umkc.edu/faculty/projects/ftrials/wilde/poemsofdouglas.htm.

Durkheim, E. (1950). *The rules of sociological method*. Glencoe, IL: The Free Press.

Field, T. (1988). Stimulation of preterm infants. *Pediatrics in Review, 10*(5), 149-154.

Fine, G. A., & Manning, P. (2003). Erving Goffman. In G. Ritzer

(Ed.), *The Blackwell companion to major contemporary social theorists*. Malden, MA: Blackwell Publishing Ltd. doi: 10.1002/9780470999912.ch3

Fredrickson, B. L. (1998). What good are positive emotions? *Review of General Psychology, 2*, 300-319.

Fredrickson, B. L. (2001). The role of positive emotions in positive psychology: The broaden-and-build theory of positive emotions. *American Psychologist, 56*(3), 218-226.

Fredrickson, B. L. (2003). The value of positive emotions. *American Scientist, 91*, 330-335.

Fredrickson, B. L., & Branigan, C. (2005). Positive emotions broaden the scope of attention and thought–action repertoires. *Cognitive Emotion, 19*, 313-332.

Fredrickson, B. L., & Joiner, T. (2002). Positive emotions trigger upward spirals toward emotional well-being. *Psychological Science, 13*, 172-175.

Gallor, S. M., & Fassinger, R. E. (2010). Social support, ethnic identity, and sexual identity of lesbians and gay men. *Journal of Gay & Lesbian Social Services, 22*, 287-315. doi:10.1080/10538720903426404

GLSENC. (2013). Gay, Straight & Lesbian Education Network, Center for Innovative Public Health Research, & Crimes against Children Research Center. Out online: The experiences of lesbian, gay, bisexual and transgender youth on the Internet. New York, NY: GLSEN.

Gergen, K.J., & Davis, K. E. (1985). *The social construction of the person*. New York: Springer-Verlag.

Goffman, I. (1963). *Stigma: Notes on the management of spoiled identity*. New York: Simon & Schuster.

Hamilton, W. D. (1964) The genetical evolution of social behaviour I and II. *Journal of Theoretical Biology, 7*, 17-52.

Hamilton, D. L., & Rose, T. L. (1980). Illusory correlation and the maintenance of stereotypical beliefs. *Journal of Personality and Social Psychology, 39*, 832-845.

Harlow, H. (1958). The nature of love. *American Psychologist, 13,* 573-685

Hechter, M., & Opp, K. D. (2001). *Social Norms,* New York: Russell Sage Foundation.

Hillier, L., & Harrison, L. (2007). Building realities less limited than their own: Young people practising same-sex attraction on the Internet. *Sexualities, 10,* 82-100. http://dx.doi.org/10.1177/1363460707072956

Hillier, L., Horsely, P., & Kurdas, C. (2004). It made me feel braver, I was no longer alone: Same sex attracted young people negotiating the pleasures and pitfalls of the Internet. In J. A. Nieto (Ed.), *Sexuality in the Pacific.* Madrid: AECI (Asociación Espanola de Coperación Internacional) and the AEEP (Asociación Espanola de Estudios del Pacífico).

Hillier, L., Mitchell, K. J., & Ybarra, M. L. (2012). The Internet as a safety net: Findings from a series of online focus groups with LGB and non-LGB young people in the U.S. *Journal of LGBT Youth, 9,* 225-246. http://dx.doi.org/10.1080/19361653.2012.684642

Kuyper, L., & Fokkema, T. (2011). Minority stress and mental health among Dutch LGBs: Examination of differences between sex and sexual orientation. *Journal of Counseling Psychology, 58,* 222-233. doi:10.1037/a0022688

Marmor, J., Bieber, I., & Gold, R. (1999). A symposium: Should homosexuality be in the APA nomenclature? In L. Gross & J. D. Woods (Eds.), *The Columbia reader on lesbians and gay men in media, society, and politics.* New York: Columbia University Press.

Maslow, A. H. (1968). *Toward a psychology of being* (2nd ed.). New York: Van Nostrand Reinhold.

McKenna, K.Y.A., & Bargh, J. A. (2000). Plan 9 from cyberspace: The implications of the internet for personality and social psychology. *Personality & Social Psychology Review,* 4, 57–75. http://dx.doi.org/10.1207/S15327957PSPR04016

Meyer, I. H. (1995). Minority stress and mental health in gay men. *Journal of Health and Social Behavior, 36*, 38-56.

Meyer, I. H. (2003). Prejudice, social stress, and mental health in lesbian, gay and bisexual populations: Conceptual issues and research evidence. *Psychological Bulletin, 129*, 674-697. doi:10.1037/0033-2909.129.5.674

Mustanski, B., Lyons, T., & Garcia, S. (2011). Internet use and sexual health of young men who have sex with men: A mixed-methods study. *Archives of Sexual Behavior, 40*, 289-300. http://dx.doi.org/10.1007/s10508-009-9596-1

Nicholas, S. K. (1995). Identity formation in gay and lesbian adolescents. PhD thesis, The Fielding Institute, DAI, Vol. 56-07B, p. 4035.

Pachankis, J. E. (2006). The psychological implications of concealing a stigma: A cognitive-affective-behavioral model. *Psychological Bulletin, 133*(2), 328-45.

Pachankis, J. E., & Goldfried, M. R. (2006). Social anxiety in young gay men. *Journal of Anxiety Disorders, 20*, 996-1015.

Perez, R. M., DeBord, K. A., & Bieschke, K. J. (Eds.). (2000). *Handbook of counseling and psychotherapy with lesbian, gay, and bisexual clients*. Washington, DC: American Psychological Association.

Raushenbush, P. B. (2014). African-American vs. gay civil rights is a false choice. Huffington Post. http://www.huffingtonpost.com/paul-raushenbush/african-american-gay-civil-rights_b_5353878.html.

Parsons, T. (1951). *The Social System*. New York: Routledge.

Parsons, T., & Shills, E. A. (1951). *Towards a general theory of action*. Cambridge, MA: Harvard University Press.

Scrivner, R. W. (1984). A model for the development of lesbian and gay identities. Paper presented at the 42nd Annual Conference of the AAMFT, San Francisco, CA.

Spitz, R. A. (1945). Hospitalism—an inquiry into the genesis of psychiatric conditions in early childhood. *Psychoanalytic Study of the Child, 1*, 53-74.

Tajfel, H., & Turner, J. C. (1986). The social identity theory of intergroup behaviour. In S. Worchel & W. G. Austin (Eds.), *Psychology of*

Intergroup Relations (pp. 7-24). Chicago, IL: Nelson-Hall.

Trivers, R. L. (1971). The evolution of reciprocal altruism. *Q. Rev. Biol., 46*, 35-57.

Troiden, R. R. (1970). Becoming homosexual: A model of gay identity acquisition. *Psychiatry, 42*, 363-372.

Troiden, R. R. (1984/85). Self, self-concept, identity, and homosexual identity: Constructs in need of definition and differentiation. *Journal of Homosexuality, 10*, 97-109.

Troiden, R. R. (1988). *Gay and lesbian identity: A sociological analysis.* Dix Hills, NY: General Hall.

Troiden, R. R. (1989). The formation of homosexual identities. *Journal of Homosexuality, 17*(1), 43-73.

Tugade, M. M., & Fredrickson, B. L. (2004). Resilient individuals use positive emotions to bounce back from negative emotional experiences. *Journal of Personality and Social Psychology, 86*, 320-333.

U.S. Supreme Court. (2015). Obergefell et al., v. Hodges, Director, Ohio Department of Health, et al. http://www.supremecourt.gov/opinions/14pdf/14-556_3204.pdf.

Walker, B. (1998). The instinct of survival. http://jrscience.wcp.muohio.edu/Research/HNatureProposalsArticles/Draft2.TheInstinctof-Survi.html.

Wilson, E. O. (2000). *Sociobiology.* Cambridge, MA: Harvard University Press.

About the Author

Dr. Jon Cabiria is a technology psychologist focused on the psychological and sociological influences of digital experiences in real-world lives. He is the sole proprietor of Teksylos, now in its 24th year, and is a technology consultant and executive coach. He helps technology leaders with a wide range of services related to company startups, product development, and leadership issues. Dr. Cabiria also is a firm believer in "giving back." Recognizing how fortunate he was to have benefited from a solid education, he "pays it forward" by bringing his expertise into the classroom, where he develops and teaches courses in the intersection of human behavior and new media technologies. Dr. Cabiria is a published author, and he is a frequent presenter and keynote speaker at many key educational and technology conferences, both domestically and internationally. He lives in Philadelphia with his dogs, cats, and a starling named Billy Bob. A believer in balance, he is at the gym several times a week, bikes 50+ miles a week, and travels often. He can be reached at jon@teksylos.com.

About the Editor

Dr. Jason Ohler is a professor emeritus, speaker, writer, teacher and cyber researcher. An early adopter of online technologies, he has been teaching online and studying the impacts of digital communities for three decades. He is author of many books and articles, and recipient of many citations and awards in the fields of technology and learning. His most recent book, *Digital Community, Digital Citizen* addresses the history, future, and ethical concerns associated with navigating our digital lifestyles. His upcoming book, *Four Big Ideas—Understanding our Innovative Selves*, considers life in a new era in which we live in two places at once—in real life, as well as in the immersive reality that exists on the other end of our smart devices—wherever we go. He is co-creator of the International Society of Technology and Education's Digital Citizenship network and has been active in the digital citizenship movement since its inception. His early work on the social impacts of technology, *Taming the Beast—Choice and Control in the Electronic Jungle*, was called by Neill Postman "the best . . . in terms of what to do about media in the education of our youth."

He serves as Professor Emeritus of Educational Technology for the University of Alaska, and currently teaches media literacy and storytelling and media for Fielding Graduate University's Media Psychology PhD program.

About Fielding Graduate University

Fielding Graduate University, headquartered in Santa Barbara, CA, was founded in 1974, and celebrated its 40th anniversary in 2014. Fielding is an accredited, nonprofit leader in blended graduate education, combining face-to-face and online learning. Its curriculum offers quality master's and doctoral degrees for professionals and academics around the world. Fielding's faculty members represent a wide spectrum of scholarship and practice in the fields of educational leadership, human and organizational development, and clinical and media psychology. Fielding's faculty serves as mentors and guides to self-directed students who use their skills and professional experience to become powerful, socially responsible leaders in their communities, workplaces, and society. For more information, please visit Fielding online at www.fielding.edu.